Be Alive as Long as You Live

Be Alive as Long as You Live

THE OLDER PERSON'S COMPLETE GUIDE TO EXERCISE FOR JOYFUL LIVING

BY
LAWRENCE J. FRANKEL AND
BETTY BYRD RICHARD

LIPPINCOTT & CROWELL, PUBLISHERS • NEW YORK

Designed by Helene Berinsky.
Photographs by Jack Tiernan.
Additional photographs by Grubb Photo Service, Inc.
Additional art supplied by Caroline Richard Rossman.

U.S. Library of Congress Cataloging in Publication Data

Frankel, Lawrence J
  Be alive as long as you live.

  Bibliography: p.
  Includes index.
  1. Aged—Health and hygiene. 2. Exercise for the
aged. I. Richard, Betty Byrd, joint author. II. Title.
RA777.6.F72 1980   613.7'1 80-10384
ISBN 0-690-01892-4

---

80 81 82 83 84 10 9 8 7 6 5 4 3 2 1

To the memory of our parents

The art of living consists of dying young—
but as late as possible!

ANONYMOUS

EVERYONE CAN USE THIS BOOK!

The exercises in this book are designed for older men and women of all shapes and sizes: for those who are active and vigorous as well as those who are more frail; for those who have always led physically active lives as well as those who have never exercised before.

Be Alive as Long as You Live is a book to present to parents, grandparents, uncles, and aunts, or to friends you love, whose years you wish to enrich with the nobility of mobility and with enhanced self-image and independence.

To the millions of elders throughout the land
May this book present a helping hand.

Contents

Acknowledgments   13
Foreword by Ernst Jokl, M.D.   15
Introduction   17
 The Challenge   21
 Exercise: The Best Possible Prescription
  for Good Health   22
 What Exercise Will Do for You   24
 About the Exercises   25
 Your Fitness Checklist   27
 My Aching Back   28
 Why the Recumbent and Sitting Positions?   29
 Breathing   30
 Suggested Background Music   31
 How to Use This Book   32
 Useful Admonitions by Hans Kraus, M.D.   34

A Pharmacopoeia of Exercises for the Older Person

PART I: FLOOR EXERCISES

A. Stretching Exercises   38
B. Neck Exercises   42
C. Shoulder and Arm Exercises   44
D. Hand, Wrist, and Finger Series   47
E. Ankle Exercises   52
F. Thigh Exercise   54

G. Abdominal Exercises 56

H. Specific Exercise to Stretch the
   Hamstring Muscles 61

I. Back-relaxing Exercises 62

J. Back Arch Support 64

K. Side-lying Exercises 65

L. Hyperextension Exercise 68

M. Gluteal Exercise 70

N. Posture and Flexibility Drills for Shoulder 71

O. Exercises on All Fours 78

P. Standing Exercises 82

PART II: CHAIR EXERCISES

A. Neck Exercises 97

B. Shoulder and Arm Exercises 99

C. Hand, Wrist, and Finger Series 102

D. Ankle Exercises 107

E. Thigh Exercises 110

F. Specific Exercise to Mildly Stretch the
   Hamstring Muscles 115

G. Abdominal Series 116

H. A Dynamic Back-relaxing Exercise 120

I. Vigorous Abdominal Exercises 122

J. Abdominal Exercise for the Sides of the Waist 126

K. Combination Abdominal and Cardiorespiratory
   Exercises 127

L. Posture and Flexibility Drills for Shoulders 129

M. Arm Flings 136

N. Exercises Standing Beside the Chair 138

PART III: BEDSIDE GYMNASTICS

A Word to the Frail Older Person   148

A. Neck Exercises   149

B. Shoulder Exercises   151

C. Arm Exercises   153

D. Finger and Thumb Exercises   156

E. Leg Raising   159

F. Back-relaxing Exercises   160

G. Abdominal Exercise   162

H. Ankle Exercise   163

I. Bicycling   164

J. Leg Raising from Side-lying Position   165

K. Gluteal Exercise   166

L. Towel Exercises   167

M. Hip Raising   175

N. Preparation for Walking   176

O. Walking   179

**PART IV: INTERVAL TRAINING EXERCISES
             FOR ENDURANCE**

Introduction   184

  Suggestions for Taking Heart Rate   185

  Resting Heart Rate   186

  Immediate Heart Rate   186

  Target Heart Rate   186

Straddle Exercises   188

Step Bench Exercise   192

Alley Cat Routine   194

Rope Skipping   196

PART V: EXERCISES FOR SPECIAL PROBLEMS

Let Your Fingers Do the Walking   200
The Balance Beam   201
Grip and Finger Exercise   204

PART VI: EXERCISES FOR RELAXATION AND PEACE OF MIND

Medicine Ball   208
A Technique for Relaxation and Serenity   209

PART VII: REFLECTIONS

A Sad Refrain   212
Vignette   214
"Fitness is ageless . . . and forever young at heart"   215
Movement—Mind and Aging!   217
The Joy of Walking   218
On Your Rocker   219
Psychology of Music and Laughter   221
Diet and Nutrition   222
Fitness Abhors Fatness   223
Breaking Icons   225

Bibliography and References   227
Index   237

Acknowledgments

First and foremost, we would like to thank the hundreds of older West Virginia men and women who have contributed to our fitness revolution, smilingly and patiently learning to perform numerous calisthenics, enhancing their lives while enriching ours. Dozens of dedicated volunteers throughout our state have given of their time selflessly, dispensing understanding, love, and compassion to the lonely, depressed, and often forgotten, teaching by precept and example the awesome functional beauty inherent in God's temple—the body.

Special thanks are due to the West Virginia Commission on Aging, the West Virginia Department of Welfare, and the West Virginia Department of Health. In addition, thanks to the Claude Worthington Benedum Foundation, without whose generous support we could not have compiled this collection of charming and lovable elders in motion.

We are especially grateful to Dorothy Frankel and Samuel J. Richard, Jr., for their understanding, interest, and encouragement.

Foreword
by Ernst Jokl, M.D., F.A.C.C.

It is with special pleasure that I accept the invitation to write the foreword to this unusual book, which represents a major contribution to the welfare of older persons. Few in the United States surpass Lawrence J. Frankel and Betty Byrd Richard in their competence and dedication as teachers in the field of exercise for older persons, as experts in the application of exercise physiology, or as trustworthy guardians of their many pupils of all ages.

The fact that gerontology—the study of the process of aging and the problems of older men and women—has now grown into a discipline of its own is largely due to observations made in physiological and medical studies of senior citizens. From these studies we now know that there are two different facets of the aging process: the decline with the years of ranges of adaptability of normal functions of the human body and the appearance of diseases which occur with increasing frequency as age advances. The latter require the attention of the physician, while exercise can modify the former. We also know today that the body's responses to exercise are fundamentally the same throughout life and that the physical and mental status of older persons who are

Dr. Jokl, the founder of sports medicine in the United States, is Professor of Allied Health, University of Kentucky Medical Center, and U.S. representative on the UNESCO International Council of Sport and Physical Education.

physically active is significantly better than that of persons of the same age who have led sedentary lives. There is no doubt that *regular exercise plus medical care significantly inhibits the aging process*.

In the past few years, Americans as a nation have become more aware than ever before of the benefits of exercise and of its importance to total health and fitness for people of all ages. In addition, much attention has recently been given to the role of exercise in improving the quality of life of older persons. This new trend is, in part, a result of the manner in which the authors of this book have interpreted their extensive empirical observations in the course of their work. Over their many years of teaching, they have demonstrated that virtually every older person is likely to benefit from exercise, including many who have never before been physically active.

Exercise maintains fitness, stimulates the mind, helps to establish social contacts, prevents premature dependence on others, and generally improves the quality of life. The low-level exercises in this book are a wonderful tool that will help millions of older men and women all across the country to lead more active, happier lives. The work of Lawrence J. Frankel and Betty Byrd Richard adds a new dimension to public and personal health.

Introduction

"To Prevent Medicine"

By chase, our long lived fathers earned their food,
Toil strung the nerves and purified the blood;
But we, their sons, a pampered race of men,
Are dwindled down to three score years and ten.
Better to use your muscles, for health unbought,
Than fee the doctors for a nauseous draught.
The wise, for cure, on exercise depend.
God never made his work for man to mend!

JOHN DRYDEN (1631–1700)

"Be Alive as Long as You Live" was the title of a paper presented at the Wingate Institute, Israel, in connection with the 10th International Congress of Gerontology held in Jerusalem. Representatives of thirty-five nations attended, with close to two thousand delegates anxious to be brought up to date on the multifaceted disciplines of biology, clinical and social medicine and on such subjects as death and dying, senile **17** dementia, hormone regulation, and aging cells, which were among the topics discussed in the more than five hundred papers presented. Very little material, if any, was directed toward improving the vigor and the quality of life of the older person.

At the second plenary session of this Congress, Dr. Nathan Shock, Chief of Gerontology of the National Institutes of Health, expressed concern about the fact that since 1900 the number of people in the United States over the age of sixty-five has grown almost four times as fast as the total population. Dr. Shock went on to note that research in the field of gerontology could "have its greatest impact by reducing the need for hospitals, nursing homes, and other institutions."

Despite the billions already allocated to research, we have in the past decade witnessed a tremendous proliferation of government-subsidized warehouses for the elderly. And it is a sad fact that almost all of us have a beloved relative or friend whose life is not as fulfilling as it could be and who is, perhaps, isolated or lonely or depressed.

It does not denigrate this research to emphasize the fact that this nation boasts almost thirty-four million people over the age of sixty and that the quality of their lives is an urgent *now* priority. We cannot continue to ignore the degenerative diseases and chronic emotional and health problems of our aging population.

What, then, *can* we do to help older people lead happier and more active and satisfying lives? A growing number of physicians involved in geriatrics believe that the best way substantially to improve the quality of life in the later years and to increase life expectancy is to *slow down* the aging process—that is, to postpone the physical symptoms of aging, such as arthritis, heart attack, hypertension, and stroke, so as to make possible many more years of vigorous, purposeful living.

Our program of low-level exercises is an effective way for the older person to remain physically active and fit and at the same time slow down the appearance of symptoms of aging or prevent them from occurring. We have taught these exercises to older men and women who have engaged in sports or other fitness activities throughout their lives as well as to those who have never exercised before, to those who are normally active as well as to those who are in some way physically restricted, to persons who have not yet experienced the symptoms of aging and who want to make sure they keep their bodies in the best possible physical condition as well as to those who, because of physical handicaps or frailness, are homebound or in nursing homes, senior centers, or institutions; and we have found time and time again that if you are active, interested, and involved—both physically and mentally—you *can* ameliorate or prevent the symptoms of old age and slow down the aging process. Equally important, our experience has shown that older people who keep physically fit not only enhance their self-image and sense of independence but also are more stimulated mentally and invariably enjoy life more. The quality of their lives improves in direct proportion to the increased fitness of their bodies.

Because of our many rewarding experiences with thousands of older men and women all across the country, we humbly offer this collection of movement improvisations to *all* older persons in the hope that, in some measure, it may help to enhance the lives of large numbers of one of our nation's greatest resources, our older citizens.

To all those who read this book, we offer our sincere wish that you may truly BE ALIVE AS LONG AS YOU LIVE.

LAWRENCE J. FRANKEL
BETTY BYRD RICHARD

THE CHALLENGE

A fit person is one who is physically and mentally alert and never slips into the insidious "senior citizen" mold, shaped by old-fashioned societal and cultural patterns.

Unfortunately, however, many older people in our country do not exercise to stay fit because they have been conditioned to believe that "society" says they should not. When these men and women withdraw from physical activities, they become more and more immobile, which invariably leads to a decline in their health and spirit and may even lead to institutionalization.

But it doesn't have to be this way. By being more active, you *can* resist the physical discomfort and unhappiness often accompanying old age and, instead, look forward to each new day with zest, vitality, and confidence.

It is never too late to "get fit"—even after years of inactivity the body responds to exercise with very little difficulty. And with exercise as your guide, you can make sure that your life will be one of health, vigor, and happiness. Take the challenge!

EXERCISE: THE BEST POSSIBLE PRESCRIPTION FOR GOOD HEALTH

A prescription for physical activity or exercise is as important as any prescription for medication. Appropriate exercise maintains the strength and tone of muscles, improves the movement of joints, stimulates healthy circulation of the blood, and aids in both digestion and elimination. Most important of all, a program of regular exercise can slow down the aging process and add years of vigorous living.

Other than looking for the secret of making gold, no other problem occupied ancient alchemists as did the search for the elixir of youth. ''How can I prolong youth?'' ''How may we delay the onset of age?'' These questions are as old as humanity.

No one has ever discovered a miraculous formula for perennial youth, but exercise has always seemed a key to this quest—the founder of medicine, Hippocrates, over 2,000 years ago declared that regular exercise is man's best friend—and we now have incontrovertible proof that exercise does indeed play the central role in maintaining optimum condition—physical, mental, and emotional—and in prolonging an active life. The significance of exercise for your general health and well-being in the later years is now so well documented by investigators all over the world that it seems senseless to ignore it.

You invite weariness and boredom, physical discomfort, depression, and even death when you do not motivate yourself to be physically and mentally active to the limit of your ability. To live effectively, with real purpose, and not merely to exist, you must be *active*. This is exercise for preventive health care.

A Gallup Poll survey of 400 persons over ninety-five years of age revealed these significant findings: They were satisfied with their lot in life, *they were physically active,* and they were remarkably happy!

Your own body is the one machine that breaks down when *not* used; it works better, unquestionably, the more you use it!

WHAT EXERCISE WILL DO FOR YOU

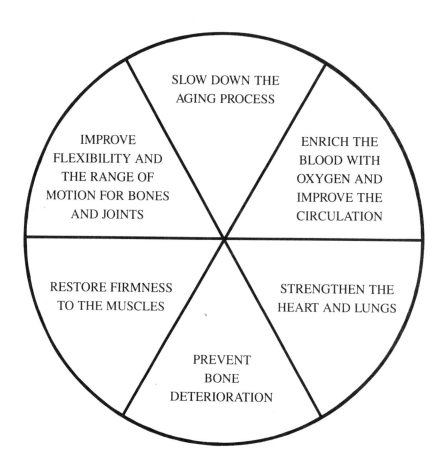

SLOW DOWN THE AGING PROCESS

ENRICH THE BLOOD WITH OXYGEN AND IMPROVE THE CIRCULATION

IMPROVE FLEXIBILITY AND THE RANGE OF MOTION FOR BONES AND JOINTS

RESTORE FIRMNESS TO THE MUSCLES

STRENGTHEN THE HEART AND LUNGS

PREVENT BONE DETERIORATION

What you prevent needs no cure

ABOUT THE EXERCISES

This book contains a series of low-level exercises designed to be used by older men and women. They are simple to do yet comprehensive and embrace every part of the body, including the head, neck, back, abdomen, arms and hands, legs, and feet. These movements improve circulation, respiration, and digestion; strengthen and tone the muscular system and the heart and lungs; improve the range of motion of all joints; and enhance general flexibility. We have placed major emphasis on exercises for peripheral circulation—that is, the circulation of the blood in the extremities—as well as on cardiovascular and cardiorespiratory exercises that limit the heart rate to a safe level of below 120 beats per minute and improve endurance without causing fatigue. There are also several relaxation and mood-elevating exercises that help relieve tension and stress and at the same time condition your body.

The exercises are designed so that they may be performed in whatever position is comfortable and convenient: in a chair, on a couch, or on a carpeted floor. They have also been adapted for those who are confined to bed, wheelchair, or walker. A minimal amount of equipment is necessary for some exercises (a 24-inch section of broomstick handle and a six-pound medicine ball); most require no equipment at all. Because of its sanguine effect on mood and tolerance, a background of instrumental music is an integral part of the exercise program.

Important: We strongly encourage you to *obtain your family physician's blessing before beginning this or any exercise program,* not because of any inherent hazard to your health but because we feel the physician plays an important role in helping to direct and maintain your physical well-being. We share the following sentiments of the eminent international exercise physiologists Per-Olof Åstrand and Kaare Rodahl:

> The question is frequently raised whether a medical examination is advisable before commencing an exercise program. Certainly anyone who is doubtful about his state of health should consult a physician. In principle, however, there is less risk in activity than in inactivity. Our opinion is that it is more advisable to pass a careful medical examination if one intends to be sedentary in order to establish whether one's state of health is good enough to stand the inactivity.*

Textbook of Work Physiology (New York: McGraw-Hill, 1976), p. 603.

YOUR FITNESS CHECKLIST

We suggest that you consult your physician before beginning this or any other exercise program. The following checklist is a useful guideline in determining your general physical condition.

Age: _____

Weight: _____

Height: _____

Blood Pressure: _____

Heart Rate: _____

Smoking Habits: _____

Medication: _____

Other: Please note if there are any contraindications or special instructions to remember before you begin exercising. _____

_____

_____

_____

_____

MY ACHING BACK

Whether they are the result of physical or psychological strain, back problems, especially pains in the lower back, are one of the most common health problems of older men and women, and we have paid special attention to them in this book.

Despite the fact that your back provides the basic support for your body and is crucial to your health and mobility, most people are unaware of the strain that daily activity places on their backs and consequently do nothing to keep them in good shape.

As we grow older and become less active, back problems are even more apparent. This is because inactivity weakens your abdominal muscles, which are the keystone to a healthy back and good posture.

Because you need strong abdominal muscles to have a strong back, we have included in this book several exercises that will help you strengthen these muscles and relieve or prevent the symptoms of chronic low back pain.

WHY THE RECUMBENT AND SITTING POSITIONS?

Many of the exercises in this book are specifically
designed to be performed from lying-down (recumbent)
or sitting positions.

The recumbent position is ideal for exercise because it
places a minimum of strain on your heart and other parts
of your body and makes it easy for you to maintain your
balance while you are concentrating on doing the
exercises. In addition, if you are lying down, you will
feel less tense and considerably less fatigued and will
therefore be able to exercise for a longer period of time
than you would otherwise.

The sitting position is similarly valuable for exercising.
When you are sitting, your pelvis is held in a fixed
position in relation to the spine, so there is minimal
strain on your lower back and on your feet and legs.
There is also less strain on your heart than there would
be if you were standing.

Exercises performed while lying down or sitting
minimize the strain on your heart and other parts of your
body, but don't assume this means that they are not
vigorous or effective—they are! They will tone your
body and help improve a variety of physical ailments
just as well as exercises that are performed from a
standing position.

BREATHING

Breathing is an important part of any exercise. Obvious as this may seem, people who are concentrating on doing an exercise often forget to breathe. *Never hold your breath while exercising.*

Learn to breathe properly: breathe out during vigorous effort and *inhale* as your muscles relax. This is especially important to remember during the abdominal and gluteal exercises. Try to establish this rhythm of breathing at the beginning so that it will soon become automatic each time you exercise.

SUGGESTED BACKGROUND MUSIC

Music has a positive effect on both mood and tolerance and is an especially helpful aid for older people who are exercising. Therefore, we recommend that you do the exercises in this book to a background of *instrumental* music, which ranges from slow to moderately lively according to the tempo of movement in the exercises. Music, of course, is a matter of individual preference, and the choice of specific musical accompaniment is up to you. The following guidelines suggest music we have found particularly appropriate:

Flexibility, range of motion, and relaxation exercises. For these exercises, try a background of waltzes, such as those of Johann Strauss, or any soft, easy-listening music—that is, instrumental music—such as the piano music of Henry Mancini. Many of Lawrence Welk's nonvocal compositions are also appropriate because they are mood-elevating.

Broomstick drills and standing exercises. As the exercises become more vigorous, use music with a somewhat more lively—but not too fast—tempo. André Kostelanetz's recording of ''Concert in the Park'' (Columbia Stereo CS 9488) or the Tijuana Brass recordings, for example, are fine accompaniments.

Endurance exercises. Slow polkas are a good background for these exercises. The music for the Alley Cat Routine is from the recording ''Lawrence Welk Presents Myron Floren's New Sound'' (Ranwood Records, RLP 8005).   **31**

HOW TO USE THIS BOOK

The exercises in this book are grouped in four main parts, and each part contains a complete series of exercises for the entire body. Please read the following descriptions to see which group of exercises is best suited to your own special needs. Be sure to do *all* the exercises in your section in the sequence presented.

PART I: *Floor Exercises*. For the vigorous, active older person.
These exercises include a variety of stretching, toning, and relaxing movements that benefit all parts of the body, from head to toe. They are designed to be performed while sitting, lying, and standing on the floor. If you have the space, we suggest that you follow this series of exercises.

PART II: *Chair Exercises*. For the vigorous, active older person who has limited space in which to exercise; also for those who are more frail or are in wheelchairs. These exercises also include a complete series of movements that stretch, tone, and relax. They are designed to be performed while sitting in or holding onto a chair. They are ideal for the active older person who, because of limited floor space, must exercise while sitting in a chair or on a couch, as well as for the more frail person who is in a wheelchair.

PART III: *Bedside Gymnastics*. For the older person who is confined to bed.

The exercises in this section encourage a holistic approach—that is, an effort on each person's part to perform the exercises with a minimum of help, so as to gradually enhance self-image and achieve an increased sense of physical and emotional independence. The exercises, the musical background, and the encourage–ment to "keep smiling" are therapeutic aids which in many cases have led to remarkably improved fitness.

PART IV: *Interval Training Exercises for Endurance*. The concluding part of the active older person's exercise session.

Active older persons should try to end each session of floor or chair exercises with one or more of the endurance exercises in this section. The interval training will be extremely helpful for those who tire easily. These exercises should *not* be attempted by those who are frail.

We recommend that you begin performing these exercises in a moderate fashion, gradually increasing the number of repetitions as your tolerance increases. This is particularly true for those who are not accustomed to exercising regularly. If at any time you begin to tire or feel fatigued, heed your body's signal to stop and rest before continuing.

USEFUL ADMONITIONS

by Hans Kraus, M.D.

Start all exercise programs with relaxing movements, then limber and stretch before any endurance regimes; finish by relaxing.

Remember to start with a few repetitions, three or four, to prevent beginning stiffness.

The slight pause between movements is to enhance relaxation.

Now you are ready to begin. . . .

A PHARMACOPOEIA OF EXERCISES FOR THE OLDER PERSON

Leit-motif

אַל תַּשְׁלִיכֵנוּ לְעֵת זִקְנָה, כִּכְלוֹת כֹּחֵנוּ אַל תַּעַזְבֵנוּ.

Al tashlichenu l'es ziknoh,
Kichlos kocheynu al ta-azvenu.

Cast me not off in the time of old age;
When my strength faileth, forsake me not.

Psalms 71:9

PART I
Floor Exercises:
For the active older person

We recommend that you do these exercises no less than 3 times a week, preferably on alternate days, and in the sequence presented. The exercises should be done to a slow, rhythmic count to avoid any jerky movements.

You should perform all the exercises in this section at least once, increasing repetitions by one each week until you reach the maximum number indicated in the text.

If you are able, we suggest that after you do these exercises you finish your session with one of the endurance exercises in Part IV.

Time: 35 to 45 minutes.

A. Stretching Exercises

To improve flexibility of hamstring muscles and lower back

1. ALTERNATE STRETCHING

Sit in erect position on floor, legs approximately 30 inches apart, hands on thighs. Reach very s-l-o-w-l-y toward the right calf, ankle, or toes, depending upon your flexibility. Keep head between arms and keep knees flat to floor. As you are reaching, *bounce very gently* to count of 4, *hold* position to count of 4, then return to starting position. Repeat on opposite side.

COUNT (bouncing *very* gently):
ONE-2-3-4 *HOLD*-2-3-4 *UP*
TWO-2-3-4 *HOLD*-2-3-4 *UP* etc.

Repetitions: 3 minimum, each side; 6 maximum.

2. REACHING THROUGH CENTER

Starting position same as No. 1.
Reach through center as far as possible, head between arms and knees flat to floor.

Count and procedure: same as No. 1.

Repetitions: 3 minimum: 6 maximum.

3. LEGS TOGETHER

Sitting in erect position, legs together, s-l-o-w-l-y reach toward calf, ankle, or toes, keeping head between arms and knees flat to floor.

Count and procedure: same as No. 1.

Repetitions: 3 minimum; 6 maximum.

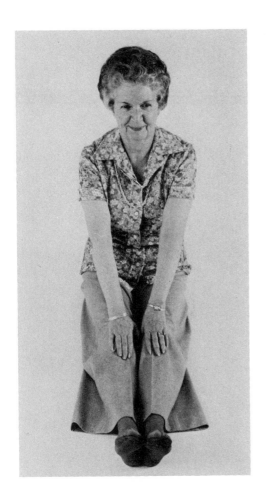 

B. Neck Exercises

To improve function and range of motion of the muscles and joints of neck and upper spine

1. HEAD BACK AND FORWARD

Sitting in erect position, s-l-o-w-l-y move head back as far as possible and s-l-o-w-l-y forward, chin toward chest.

COUNT: *ONE* (head back) *AND* (head forward, chin toward chest)
TWO (back) *AND* (forward) etc.

Repetitions: 5 each direction.

2. EAR TOWARD SHOULDER

Move head alternately, right to left, keeping shoulders perfectly still; right ear toward right shoulder, left ear toward left shoulder.

COUNT: *ONE* (to the right) *AND* (to the left)
TWO (right) *AND* (to the left) etc.

Repetitions: 5 each direction.

3. HEAD TURNED TO LOOK OVER SHOULDER

Alternately look over right and left shoulder.

COUNT: same as No. 2.

Repetitions: 5 each direction.

C. Shoulder and Arm Exercises

To enhance and improve range of motion in the shoulders and to strengthen the deltoid muscles

1. SHOULDER SHRUGS

Sitting tall, arms at sides, shrug shoulders up toward ears and down.

COUNT:
ONE (up) *AND* (down)
TWO (up) *AND* (down) etc.

Repetitions: 5.

2. SHOULDER ROTATIONS

Shrug and rotate shoulders forward, s-l-o-w-l-y, making 5 complete rotations. Then rotate shoulders backward.

COUNT (slowly):
ONE (forward)
AND (completion of rotation)
TWO (forward)
AND (completion of rotation) etc.

Repetitions: 5 each direction.

3. ARM CIRCLES

Extend arms horizontally sideward, palms down; stretch arms outward. Do not bend elbows; hold head in good posture. Rotate arms *from the shoulders,* making very small circles, s-l-o-w-l-y.

COUNT: same as No. 2.

Repetitions: 10 complete rotations forward: 10 rotations backward.

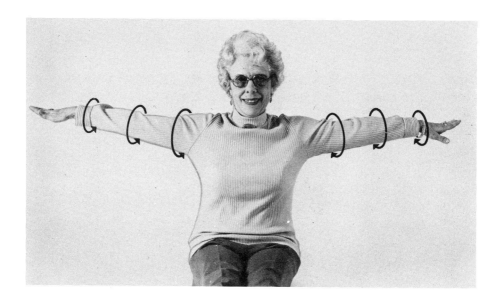

D. Hand, Wrist, and Finger Series

To improve range of motion and flexibility; often ameliorates arthritis in these areas

1. HAND ROTATION

Grasping right wrist with left hand, *s-l-o-w-l-y* rotate right hand, *making large complete circles,* keeping palm facing down. Repeat for opposite hand.

COUNT:
ONE (to the right)
AND (completion of rotation)
TWO (to the right)
AND (completion of rotation) etc.

Repetitions: 10 clockwise (for each hand): 10 counterclockwise.

 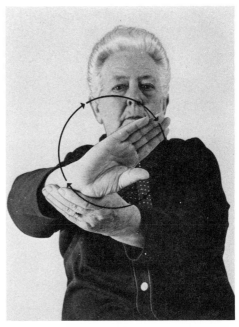

2. FINGER STRETCHING

With palm of right hand facing down, gently force fingers back toward forearm, using left hand for leverage; then place left hand on top and force fingers down. Repeat with opposite hand.

COUNT:
ONE (pull fingers back)
AND (push fingers down)
TWO (pull fingers back)
AND (push fingers down) etc.

Repetitions: 5 each direction.

3. FINGER FLEXION AND EXTENSION

Extend arms forward. Clench fists tightly; then extend fingers slowly.

COUNT:
ONE (clench) *AND* (extend)
TWO (clench) *AND* (extend) etc.

Repetitions: 10.

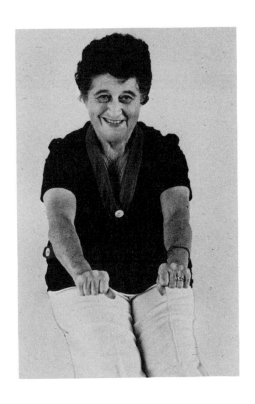 

4. FINGER SPREADING

With arms straight out, palms facing down, spread fingers wide apart and then bring them together.

COUNT:
ONE (apart) *AND* (together)
TWO (apart) *AND* (together) etc.

Repetitions: 5.

5. THUMB ROTATIONS

Rotate both thumbs forward s-l-o-w-l-y: then repeat in reverse.

COUNT:
ONE (forward)
AND (completion of rotation)
TWO (forward)
AND (completion of rotation) etc.

Repetitions: 5 rotations each direction.

E. Ankle Exercises

To improve range of motion and flexibility in the ankle joint

1. FOOT ROTATIONS

Cross right leg over left knee and rotate right foot clockwise s-l-o-w-l-y, making large complete circles. Then rotate foot counterclockwise. Repeat with left foot.

COUNT:
ONE (to the right)
AND (completion of rotation)
TWO (to the right)
AND (completion of rotation) etc.

Repetitions: 10 clockwise (for each foot); 10 counterclockwise.

2. ANKLE FLEXION AND EXTENSION

With legs extended, flex ankles toward shin and then extend.

COUNT:
ONE (flex) *AND* (extend)
TWO (flex) *AND* (extend) etc.

Repetitions: 10.

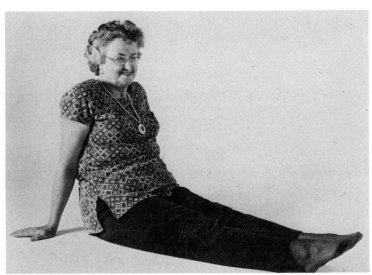

F. Thigh Exercise

To tone and strengthen inside and outside thigh muscles

Starting with knees bent and together, feet flat to floor, hands on outside of knees, separate knees, pushing against resistance of hands, to a slow count of 5. Then, with knees widely separated, place palms of hands on

inside of knees and bring knees together against resistance of hands to slow reverse count of 5.

COUNT:
ONE-2-3-4-5 (knees separated) *AND*
FIVE-4-3-2-1 (knees together)
TWO-2-3-4-5 (knees separated) *AND*
FIVE-4-3-2-1 (knees together) etc.

Repetitions: 5.

G. Abdominal Exercises
To strengthen the upper and lower abdominal muscles

IMPORTANT: *While you are doing one of these abdominal exercises, exhale forcefully with the effort; never hold your breath. Blow out through mouth as though blowing out a candle.*

1. SIT-UP FOR THE UNTRAINED INDIVIDUAL

From back-lying position, hands on thighs with arms extended, raise head and shoulders up as far as possible—very s-l-o-w-l-y. Keep chin on chest. Exhale with the effort and return to starting position.

Repetitions: 5 minimum; 10 maximum.

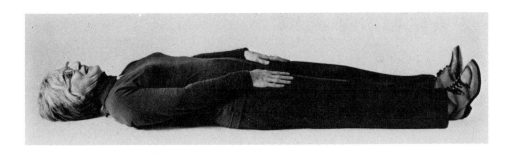

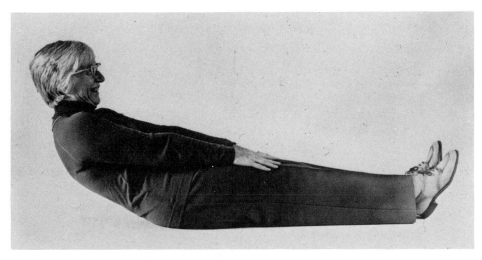

2. FLEXED KNEE SIT-UP USING STALL BAR

Stall bars are usually gymnasium apparatus; if unavailable, hook toes under couch or heavy chair.

Hook toes under stall bar or piece of furniture, with knees flexed and arms extended behind head. Pull up to sitting position, exhale with the effort, and return very s-l-o-w-l-y to starting position.

Repetitions: 5 minimum: 10 maximum.

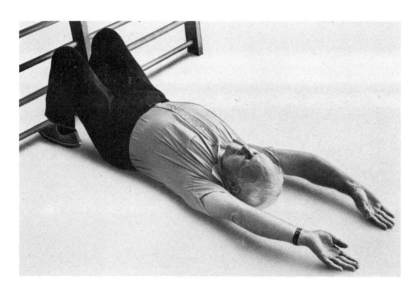

3. HALF SIT-UPS

For those who have performed the previous exercises without difficulty, it is possible to perform this exercise without hooking your toes.

From position lying on back, extend arms and legs. Reach up and forward to touch fingers to *beginning* of knee caps. *Exhale with the effort* and return to starting position.
Start with no more than 3 repetitions, gradually increasing by one each week.

Repetitions: 10 maximum.

4. SIT-BACK

This abdominal exercise is more vigorous than the preceding ones.

Hook toes under stall bar with knees flexed and hands clasped behind head. Pull up to sitting position, exhaling with the effort. Going back very s-l-o-w-l-y, return to starting position.

Repetitions: 5 maximum.

H. Specific Exercise to Stretch the Hamstring Muscles

To improve flexibility of the muscles behind the knee, make movements more graceful, reduce loss of balance, improve mobility, and add a youthful gait

Lie on back with arms at sides, palms facing down. Bend *left knee* and extend right leg. Raise right leg up as far as possible and return to starting position. Repeat same procedure, bending right knee and raising left leg upward and backward.

COUNT:
ONE (up) *AND* (down)
TWO (up) *AND* (down) etc.

Repetitions: 5 minimum (for each leg); 10 maximum.

I. Back-relaxing Exercises
To relax the muscles of the lower back and reduce stiffness and tension in that area

1. KNEE TO CHEST

Lying on your back, legs straight, arms at sides, raise the right knee, grasp it with both hands, and pull toward chest. At the same time, bring *forehead toward knee,* keeping chin on chest; return to starting position. Repeat same exercise, bringing left knee to chest.

COUNT:
ONE (right knee and chin to chest)
AND (starting position)
TWO (right knee and chin to chest)
AND (starting position) etc.

Repetitions: 5 minimum (for each knee); 10 maximum.

2. BOTH KNEES TO CHEST

From same starting position as No. 1, grasp both knees and pull toward chest. Bring forehead toward knees, keeping chin on chest; return to starting position.

Repetitions and count: same as No. 1.

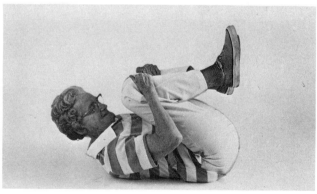

J. Back Arch Support

To strengthen the upper back muscles and to firm the back of the upper arms

Starting from sitting position, upper body erect, hands behind and slightly to the sides, raise hips from floor until body is perfectly straight, with the head back. HOLD to count of 4; return to starting position. Repeat exercise 3 times, adding one repetition each week.

COUNT:
UP-2-3-4 *AND DOWN*
TWO-2-3-4 *AND DOWN* etc.

Repetitions: 10 maximum.

K. Side-lying Exercises

To strengthen and improve flexibility of thighs, hips, and side-of-waist muscles

NOTE: *The following three exercises should be performed lying on the right side and then repeated, in the same sequence, lying on the left side.*

1. LEG RAISING

Lie on right side with head resting comfortably on extended arm, other arm and hand to the side in front of waist (to maintain balance), legs together, and back slightly arched. Raise left leg upward as far as possible. *Do not bend knee.* Return to starting position.

COUNT:
ONE (raise left leg up); *AND* (return to starting position)
TWO (raise left leg up)
AND (return to starting position) etc.

Repetitions: 5 minimum; 10 maximum.

2. SCISSORS KICK

Lying on right side, kick legs vigorously back and forth in scissors fashion. Do not bend knees.

Repetitions: 10.

3. SIDE STRETCH

Raise upper body and legs simultaneously, looking over shoulder and behind hips toward heels. *Hold* this position to count of 4 and return to starting position. Do not bend knees.
Start with 3 repetitions, increasing one each week.

COUNT:
UP-2-3-4 *AND DOWN*
TWO-2-3-4 *AND DOWN* etc.

Repetitions: 10 maximum.

L. Hyperextension Exercise
To strengthen upper and lower back and to improve flexibility of the spine

Starting from prone position, arms and legs fully extended, head down, raise arms, legs, and head simultaneously, arching the entire body *without bending legs or arms*. Maintaining this same arch position, extend arms sideward; then extend arms forward (holding momentarily), and return to starting position (head down).

Do 3 times; add one repetition each week.

This is a four-count exercise.

COUNT:
ONE (raise arms, legs, and head simultaneously)
TWO (extend arms sideward)
THREE (extend arms forward)
FOUR (down to starting position)

TWO-2-3-4
THREE-2-3-4
FOUR-2-3-4 etc.

Repetitions: 5 maximum.

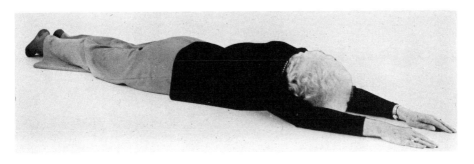

M. Gluteal Exercise

To improve circulation in rectal sphincter
(often improves hemorrhoidal conditions)

IMPORTANT: *Remember to inhale and exhale normally during this exercise.*

Prone position, resting head on arms, legs straight, toes together, heels outward. To a slow count of four, tighten gluteal (buttock) muscles, bringing heels together; hold for a slow count of four; and relax. (Tighten these muscles as though you were given an enema and told to hold the water.)

COUNT:
ONE-2-3-4; HOLD-2-3-4; Relax
TWO-2-3-4; HOLD-2-3-4; Relax etc.

Repetitions: 10.

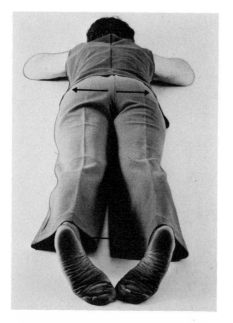 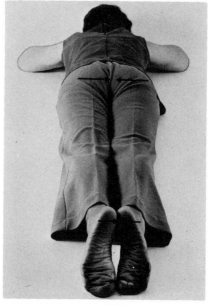

N. Posture and Flexibility Drills for Shoulder

To enhance posture and strengthen hand muscles

1. Use a 24-inch portion of broomstick. Sitting in erect position, arms straight and resting on thighs, grasp broomstick handle. Hands should be shoulder width apart. Raise broomstick forward and up to shoulder level and return to starting position.

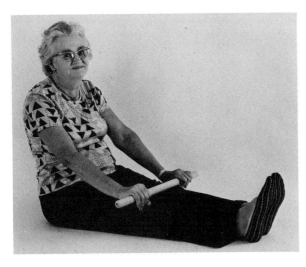

COUNT:
ONE (up)
AND (down)
TWO (up)
AND (down) etc.

Repetitions: 10.

2. Reach forward and upward over head, keeping arms close to ears—stretch hard, and return to thighs.

Repetitions and count: same as No. 1.

3. Bring broomstick to chest; vigorously push forward and backward.

COUNT:
ONE (forward) *AND* (back)
TWO (forward) *AND* (back) etc.

Repetitions: 10.

4. Starting with broomstick on knees, arms extended, bring broomstick forward, up, and behind neck; return to starting position.

COUNT:
ONE (broomstick
        behind neck)
AND (starting position)
TWO (broomstick
        behind neck)
AND (starting position) etc.

Repetitions: 10.

5. With broomstick behind neck, twist from waist, right to left in a continuous motion.

COUNT:
ONE (twist to the right)
AND (twist to the left)
TWO (to the right)
AND (to the left) etc.

Repetitions: 5 minimum each direction; 10 maximum.

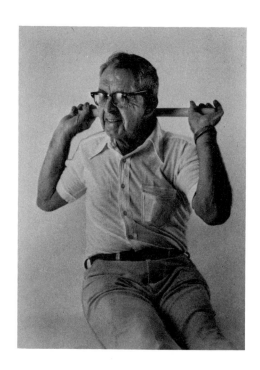

6. Hold broomstick at shoulder level, arms extended. Using the *first joint* of the fingers and thumbs, roll stick forward 10 times and then in reverse direction 10 times. This is an excellent finger exercise.

7. Hold broomstick vertically, grasping tightly; wring s-l-o-w-l-y and vigorously, 10 times.

8. Hold broomstick out at shoulder level, arms extended. Cross right arm over left, then left over right.
Do not bend arms.

COUNT:
ONE (right over left)
AND (left over right)
TWO (right over left)
AND (left over right) etc.

Repetitions: 10.

9. Hold broomstick between palms of hands, arms extended horizontally at shoulder level. Push in at both ends with palms; then turn stick vertically, with *left* hand on top, and push on both ends. Turn broomstick horizontally again and push in, then turn vertically and push, this time with *right* hand on top.

COUNT:
ONE (push horizontally)
AND (turn clockwise and push vertically)
TWO (turn back to horizontal and push)
AND (turn counterclockwise and push vertically) etc.

Repetitions: 10.

10. The ultimate in flexibility.

O. Exercises on All Fours

To improve flexibility of the spine and slightly tone the abdominal muscles; also to improve body awareness and balance and strengthen upper and lower back

1. CAT EXERCISE

Support weight on hands and knees, keeping arms straight (do not bend elbows), with head up and back slightly arched.

Lower head toward chest, at the same time pulling abdominal muscles up toward backbone s-l-o-w-l-y; *do not rock back and forth, do not hold the breath, do not bend elbows.* Hold this position for count of four. RELAX to starting position (back arched and head up).

COUNT (slowly):
ONE-2-3-4 (head down toward chest, back arched)
HOLD-2-3-4
RELAX (starting position)
TWO-2-3-4
HOLD-2-3-4
RELAX etc.

Repetitions: 5.

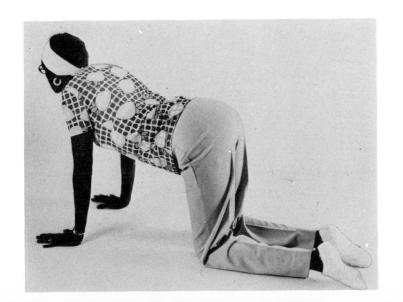

2. KNEE FLEXION, EXTENSION, AND SCALE

Supporting weight on hands and knees as in cat exercise, with arms straight and head up, flex *right* knee toward chest, the *forehead* going toward the knee, the *head down* with chin on chest. Now extend *right* leg backward and upward as far as possible, *at the same time raising head;* then extend *left arm* forward and upward. (This position is called scale. It is a challenging

gymnastic movement for the older person.) Return to starting position and perform with *left* leg and *right* arm.

COUNT:

FLEX (right knee to chest)

EXTEND (right leg backward and upward)

SCALE (extend left arm forward and upward)

CHANGE (starting position) etc.

Repetitions: 5 each side, alternating right and left.

P. Standing Exercises

1. LEG LUNGING
To strengthen the muscles of the upper thighs and firm the buttocks

Standing with hands on hips, lunge forward on right foot, keeping back leg straight, arms horizontally forward. Flex forward leg to a right angle (never more), then return to starting position.
The upper body should always be vertical; do not lean forward. Repeat on opposite leg.

COUNT:
ONE (lunge forward) *AND* (return to erect position)
TWO (forward) *AND* (return) etc.

Repetitions: 3 minimum, each leg; 5 maximum.

2. KNEE TO CHEST
To improve balance, relax low back, and firm abdomen

For beginners with poor balance; hold hands with partner as illustrated, raise right knee toward chest, and return to starting position. For those able to maintain balance, perform same knee-to-chest exercise without benefit of partner. Repeat with left knee.

COUNT:
ONE (up) *AND* (down)
TWO (up) *AND* (down) etc.

Repetitions: 3 minimum, each knee; 10 maximum.

3. HALF KNEE BEND
To strengthen thigh muscles without over-stretching knee joint

Standing erect with heels together and toes pointed outward, squat to a half knee bend, keeping back perfectly straight.
This exercise may also be performed holding hands within a group.

COUNT:
ONE (down) *AND* (up)
TWO (down) *AND* (up) etc.

Repetitions: 5 minimum; 10 maximum.

4. RAG DOLL
A relaxing exercise for the muscles of the lower back, inhibiting tension and slightly stretching the hamstrings

Standing erect, with legs approximately 12 to 14 inches apart, bend s-l-o-w-l-y forward from waist. KEEP HEAD BETWEEN ARMS AND DO NOT BEND KNEES. Drop as far as possible without effort (relaxing just as if you were a rag doll), utilizing only the pull of

gravity to move you forward and down; swing arms loosely. Then return to starting position.

COUNT (slowly):
ONE (bend over slowly and swing arms)
AND (return to erect position)
TWO (bend over slowly and swing arms)
AND (return to erect position) etc.

Repetitions: 5 minimum; 10 maximum.

5. SIDE BENDS

To strengthen and improve flexibility of muscles at sides of waist

Standing with legs together, arms at sides, erect position, step out to the side with *right foot*, simultaneously extending *right arm* upward and close to the ear and maintaining erect posture. *Do not lean forward.* Lean body toward left side and stretch as far as possible *without forcing the motion*. Continue this

stretching, reaching as far as possible, and then return to erect starting position. Repeat on opposite side.

COUNT(slowly):
ONE (step to right, right arm up, lean left)
AND (return to starting position)
TWO (step to left, left arm up, lean right)
AND (return to starting position) etc.

Repetitions: 3 minimum each side; 6 maximum; alternating right and left.

6. ARM CIRCLES
To enhance range of motion and circulation in shoulder

With arms extended and crossed in front of thighs and with feet slightly apart, circle both arms, crossing in front of face. Bring arms down laterally (sideways) with continuous movement. Repeat, circling in opposite direction.

COUNT:
ONE (circle arms)
AND (completion of rotation)
TWO (circle arms)
AND (completion of circle) etc.

Repetitions: 10, each direction.

7. ARM FLINGS
To improve flexibility of shoulders and relieve tension in these muscles

Standing in erect position, extend arms horizontally forward at shoulder height, crossing at wrists, right arm over left. Fling arms outward and backward as far as possible, maintaining their horizontal position. *Never let arms drop below shoulder level.* Then immediately fling arms horizontally forward again, crossing *the left arm over the right.* Continue this motion vigorously and rhythmically, backward and forward, alternating left over right and right over left. Do not bend elbows.

COUNT:
ONE (arms back)
AND (arms forward, right over left)
TWO (arms back)
AND (arms forward, left over right) etc.

Repetitions: 10.

8. HIP ROTATIONS
To make hip joints more flexible and stretch hip rotators

With hands on hips, feet slightly apart, rotate hips in a large circle, first to right, then to left. Keep head upright.

COUNT:
ONE (rotate hips to the right)
AND (completion of rotation)
TWO (rotate hips to the left)
AND (completion of rotation) etc.

Repetitions: 5 rotations each direction.

Please continue with the interval training exercises on page 183.

PART II

Chair Exercises:

For the active older person who has a
limited space in which to exercise and
for the person who is either frail or
confined to a wheelchair

*The exercises in this section may be modified from the
somewhat vigorous to the extremely mild, to
accommodate both the active older person who, because
of space limitations, is exercising from a chair or couch
and the more frail individual who is in a wheelchair,
nursing home, or nutrition site or who is homebound.
Do the exercises to a slow, rhythmic count; avoid any
jerky motions. Whenever possible, use a hard-back
chair while performing these exercises.*

There are three positions used in the chair exercises:
Position A—Sitting back in the chair
Position B—Sitting in the middle of the chair
Position C—Sitting to the front of the chair

Active older persons: *We recommend that you do these
exercises no less than 3 times a week, preferably on
alternate days, and in the sequence presented. You
should perform all the exercises in this section at least
once, increasing repetitions by one each week until you*

reach the maximum number indicated in the text. If you are able, we suggest that after you do these exercises, you finish your session with one or more of the endurance exercises in Part IV.

Persons who are frail or confined to wheelchairs: *We recommend that you perform these exercises once a day, five days a week, and in the sequence presented. You should perform all the exercises in this section at least once, increasing repetitions by one each week until you reach the maximum number indicated in the text. Those who are in wheelchairs should do only the exercises that are designed to be performed while sitting in a chair.*

Time: 35 to 45 minutes.

A. Neck Exercises

To improve function and range of motion of the muscles and joints of neck and upper spine

1. HEAD BACK AND FORWARD

Position A
Sitting erect, good posture, s-l-o-w-l-y move head back as far as possible and s-l-o-w-l-y forward, chin toward chest.

COUNT:
ONE (head back) *AND* (head forward)
TWO (back) *AND* (forward) etc.

Repetitions: 5 each direction.

2. EAR TOWARD SHOULDER

Position A
Move head alternately, right to left, keeping shoulders perfectly still; right ear toward right shoulder, left ear toward left shoulder.

COUNT:
ONE (to the right)
AND (to the left)
TWO (right)
AND (left) etc.

Repetitions: 5 each direction.

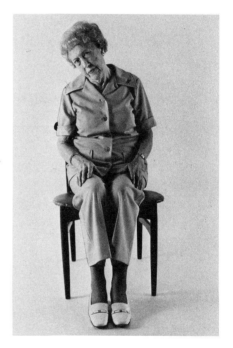

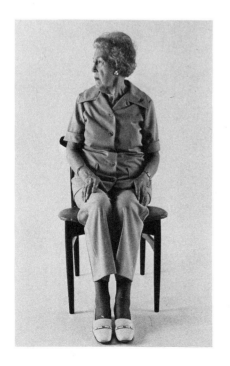

3. HEAD TURNED TO LOOK OVER SHOULDER

Position A
Alternately look over right and left shoulder.

COUNT: Same as No. 2.

Repetitions: 5 each direction.

B. Shoulder and Arm Exercises

To enhance and improve range of motion in the shoulders and to strengthen the deltoid muscles

1. SHOULDER SHRUGS

Position A
Sitting tall, hands on thighs, shrug shoulders up toward ears and down.

COUNT:
ONE (up) *AND* (down)
TWO (up) *AND* (down) etc.

Repetitions: 5.

2. SHOULDER ROTATIONS

Position A
Shrug and rotate shoulders forward, s-l-o-w-l-y, making 5 complete rotations. Then rotate shoulders backward.

COUNT (slowly):
ONE (forward)
AND (completion of rotation)
TWO (forward)
AND (completion of rotation) etc.

Repetitions: 5 each direction.

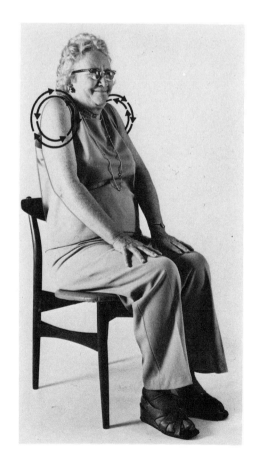

3. ARM CIRCLES

Position A
Extend arms horizontally sideward, palms down; stretch arms outward. Do not bend elbows; hold head in good posture. Rotate arms *from the shoulders,* making very small circles, s-l-o-w-l-y.

COUNT: same as No. 2.

Repetitions: 10 complete rotations forward; 10 rotations backward.

C. Hand, Wrist, and Finger Series

To improve range of motion and flexibility; often ameliorates arthritis in these areas

1. HAND ROTATIONS

Position A
Grasping right wrist with left hand, s-l-o-w-l-y rotate right hand, *making large complete circles*, keeping palm facing down. Repeat on opposite hand.

COUNT:
ONE (to the right)
AND (completion of rotation)
TWO (to the right)
AND (completion of rotation) etc.

Repetitions: 10 clockwise; 10 counterclockwise.

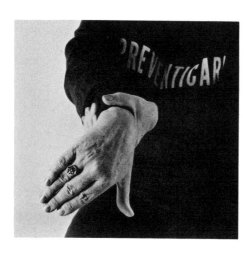 

2. FINGER STRETCHING

Position A
With palm of right hand facing down, gently force fingers back toward forearm, using left hand for leverage; then place left hand on top and force fingers down. Repeat with opposite hand.

COUNT:
ONE (pull fingers back)
AND (push fingers down)
TWO (back)
AND (down) etc.

Repetitions: 5 each direction.

3. FINGER FLEXION AND EXTENSION

Position A
Extend arms forward. Clench fists tightly; then extend fingers.

COUNT:
ONE (clench) *AND* (extend)
TWO (clench) *AND* (extend) etc.

Repetitions: 10.

4. FINGER SPREADING

Position A
With arms extended, palms facing down, spread fingers wide apart and then bring them together.

COUNT:
ONE (apart) *AND* (together)
TWO (apart) *AND* (together) etc.

Repetitions: 5.

5. THUMB ROTATIONS

Position A

Rotate both thumbs forward s-l-o-w-l-y; then repeat in reverse.

COUNT:
ONE (forward)
AND (completion of rotation)
TWO (forward)
AND (completion of rotation)

Repetitions: 5 rotations each direction.

D. Ankle Exercises

To improve range of motion and flexibility in the ankle joint

1. FOOT ROTATIONS

Position A
Cross right leg over left knee and rotate right foot clockwise s-l-o-w-l-y, making large complete circles. Then rotate foot counterclockwise. Repeat with left foot.

COUNT:
ONE (to the right)
AND (completion of rotation)
TWO (to the right)
AND (completion of rotation) etc.

Repetitions: 10 clockwise (each foot); 10 counterclockwise.

2. ANKLE EXERCISE

Position A
Turn ankles outward so that soles of feet face each other, then evert position as far as possible.

COUNT:
ONE (invert: soles of feet toward each other)
AND (evert: reverse position)
TWO (invert)
AND (evert) etc.

Repetitions: 5 each direction.

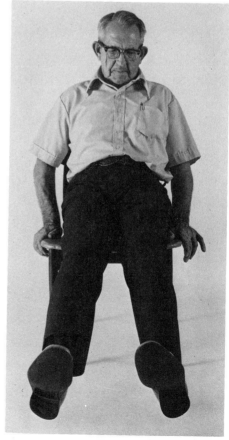

3. ANKLE FLEXION AND EXTENSION

Position A
With legs extended, flex ankles toward shin and then extend.

COUNT:
ONE (flex) *AND* (extend)
TWO (flex) *AND* (extend) etc.

Repetitions: 5.

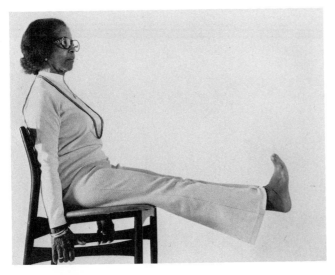

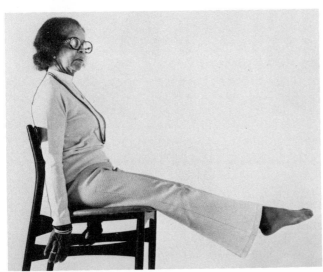

E. Thigh Exercises

To tone and strengthen inside and outside thigh muscles

Position C

1. Starting with knees bent and together, feet flat to floor, hands on outside of knees, separate knees, pushing against resistance of hands, to a slow count of 5. Then,

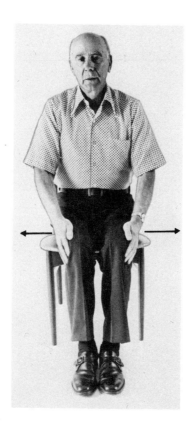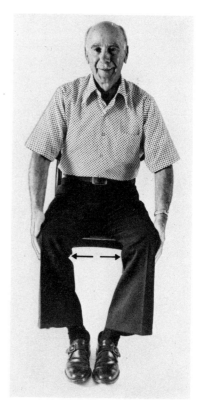

with knees widely separated, place palms of hands on inside of knees and bring knees together against resistance of hands to a slow reverse count of 5.

COUNT:
ONE-2-3-4-5 (knees separated) *and*
FIVE-4-3-2-1 (knees together)
TWO-2-3-4-5 (knees separated) *and*
FIVE-4-3-2-1 (knees together) etc.

Repetitions: 5.

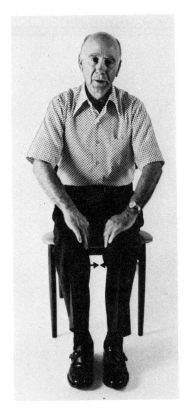

Position B or C

2. Place ankle of right foot on top of left knee; then place both hands on top of right knee and gently force downward to a count of 3, at the same time elevating the left knee by raising the heel of the left foot from the floor. Hold to count of 3; then relax. Repeat opposite side.

COUNT:
ONE-2-3; *HOLD*-2-3; *RELAX*
TWO-2-3; *HOLD*-2-3; *RELAX* etc.

Repetitions: 3 on each side.

3. QUADRICEP EXERCISE

The quadriceps are muscles of the upper thigh which practically support the weight of the body. Quadricep muscles are the key to strong and flexible knees.

Position C
Place hands on thighs, lean very slightly forward, and rise to erect position. From the erect position, s-l-o-w-l-y start sitting down, bending the knees

gradually, keeping the back straight, and counting by seconds—one-thousand-and-ONE, one-thousand-and-TWO, one-thousand-and-THREE, etc.—until you reach sitting position at the count of one-thousand-and-TEN.

Repetitions: 1 is sufficient for the beginner. Add one repetition each week until you are able to do the maximum of 5.

  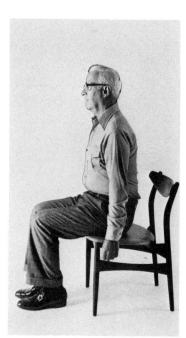

F. Specific Exercise to Mildly Stretch the Hamstring Muscles

To improve flexibility of the muscles behind the knee and add grace to your movements

Position C
Sit toward front of chair, upper back touching back of chair and hands holding to sides. Raise right leg up as far as possible and return to starting position. Repeat with opposite leg.

COUNT:
ONE (up) *AND* (down)
TWO (up) *AND* (down) etc.

Repetitions: 5 for each leg.

G. Abdominal Series

Alternate periods of exercise and relaxation to strengthen the abdominal muscles

1. DOUBLE LEG CIRCLES

Position C
With legs straight and together and upper body to back of chair, grasp both sides of chair and s-l-o-w-l-y execute large circles, clockwise, then counterclockwise.

COUNT (slowly):
ONE (to the right)
AND (completion of rotation)
TWO (to the right)
AND (completion of rotation) etc.

Repetitions: 2 minimum, each direction; 5 maximum.

2. RAG DOLL
A passive relaxing exercise for the muscles of the lower back

Position C

Sitting toward front of chair, legs approximately 12 inches apart, bend s-l-o-w-l-y forward from waist. Keeping chin on chest, drop as far as possible without

effort (relaxing just as if you were a rag doll), utilizing only the pull of gravity to move you forward and down; swing arms loosely. Then return to starting position.

COUNT (slowly):
ONE (bend forward, swing arms *loosely*)
AND (up)
TWO (bend forward, swing arms *loosely*)
AND (up) etc.

Repetitions: 3.

3. REVERSE LEG CIRCLES

Position C
With both legs fully extended and together, upper body to back of chair, raise legs as high as possible and rotate them in opposite directions in a continuous motion. Then reverse directions of each leg and repeat.

COUNT:
UP–Out-down-together and
TWO–Out-down-together etc.

REVERSE COUNT:
DOWN–Out-up-together and
TWO–Out-up-together etc.

Repetitions: 2 minimum, each direction; 5 maximum.

H. A Dynamic
Back-relaxing Exercise

Position B or C

With upper back leaning to back of chair, grasp right knee with both hands and pull toward chest; simultaneously bring forehead toward knee, hold momentarily, then return to starting position. Repeat opposite side. Then grasp both knees and pull toward chest, keeping head erect.

COUNT:
ONE (right knee toward chest)
AND (starting position)
TWO (right knee toward chest)
AND (starting position) etc.

Repetitions: 5 minimum for each exercise; 10 maximum.

I. Vigorous Abdominal Exercises

IMPORTANT: *Remember to inhale and exhale normally during these exercises.*

Position C
These are a more vigorous type of abdominal exercise than those described in group G. We recommend that in the beginning you do only 1 or 2 repetitions, gradually adding one each week until you are able to do the maximum of 5.

1. FLEX—EXTEND—FLEX—DOWN

Position C
With upper back touching back of chair and hands
holding onto sides of chair, bring both knees toward
chest, straighten legs outward, bring toward chest again,
and return to starting position.

COUNT:
FLEX-extend-flex-down
TWO-extend-flex-down etc.
Relax—Rag Doll (see page 117.)

Repetitions: 1 minimum; 5 maximum.

2. FLEX—EXTEND—SPREAD—TOGETHER—FLEX—DOWN

Same position as No. 1, this time spreading legs wide apart after flexing and extending them.

COUNT:
FLEX-extend-spread-together-flex-down
TWO-extend-spread-together-flex-down etc.
Relax—Rag Doll

Repetitions: 3.

J. Abdominal Exercise for the Sides of the Waist

Position B

Sitting erect, with feet flat on floor, arms at sides, and buttocks flat to chair, extend right arm upward (reach for ceiling, keeping the arm close to head), lean body toward left side, and stretch as far as possible without forcing the motion. Alternate with opposite side.

COUNT:
ONE (right arm up, lean left)
AND (return to starting position)
TWO (left arm up, lean right)
AND (return to starting position) etc.

Repetitions: 3 minimum, each side; 5 maximum.

K. Combination Abdominal and Cardiorespiratory Exercises

These exercises should be performed at a reasonably fast cadence.

1. BICYCLING

Position C
Raise both knees toward chest and perform pedaling movements as if riding a bicycle.

Repetitions: 10 forward; 10 backward.

2. SCISSORS KICK

Position C
Extend both legs forward; vigorously and alternately kick up and down in scissors fashion.

Repetitions: 10.

3. CROSS OVER

Position C
Extend legs forward; vigorously cross right leg over left, then left over right.

Repetitions: 10.

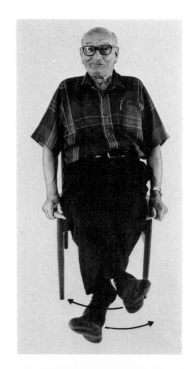

L. Posture and Flexibility Drills for Shoulders

To enhance posture and strengthen hand muscles

Position A
1. Use a 24-inch portion of broomstick. Sitting in erect position, hold broomstick at shoulder width; rest hands on thighs. Raise broomstick forward and up to shoulder level; return to starting position.

COUNT:
ONE (up) *AND* (down)
TWO (up) *AND* (down) etc.

Repetitions: 10.

2. Reach forward and upward over head, keeping arms close to ears—stretch hard, and return to thighs.

Repetitions and count: same as No. 1

3. Bring broomstick to chest; vigorously push forward and backward.

COUNT:
ONE (forward) *AND* (back to chest)
TWO (forward) *AND* (back) etc.

Repetitions: 10.

4. With hands resting on thighs, bring broomstick forward, up, and behind neck; return to thighs.

COUNT:
ONE (broomstick behind neck)
AND (return to thighs)
TWO (broomstick behind neck)
AND (return to thighs)

Repetitions: 10.

5. With broomstick behind neck, twist from waist, right to left, in a continuous motion.

COUNT:
ONE (twist to the right)
AND (twist to the left)
TWO (to the right)
AND (to the left) etc.

Repetitions: 5 minimum, each direction; 10 maximum.

6. Hold broomstick at shoulder level, arms extended. Using the *first joint* of the fingers and thumbs, roll stick forward 10 times and then in reverse direction 10 times. This is an excellent finger exercise.

7. Grasping tightly, hold broomstick vertically; wring s-l-o-w-l-y and vigorously, 10 times.

8. Hold broomstick at shoulder level, arms extended. Cross right arm over left, then left arm over right. *Do · not bend arms.*

COUNT:
ONE (right over left)
AND (left over right)
TWO (right over left)
AND (left over right) etc.

Repetitions: 10.

9. Hold broomstick between palms of hands, arms extended horizontally at shoulder level. Push in on stick at both ends, then turn it to vertical position (*left* hand on top) and exert similar pressure. Turn to horizontal position, exert pressure on both ends; then to vertical position again with *right* hand on top, exerting pressure.

COUNT:
ONE (push horizontally)
AND (turn clockwise and push vertically)
TWO (turn back to horizontal and push)
AND (turn counterclockwise and push vertically) etc.

Repetitions: 10.

M. Arm Flings

To improve flexibility of shoulders and relieve tension in these muscles

Position B

Sitting in erect position, extend arms sideward horizontally, reaching as far as possible and keeping arms at shoulder level. *Never let arms drop below shoulder level.* Fling arms forward horizontally, crossing one arm over the other (left over right). Then

immediately fling arms sideward again, keeping them at shoulder level. Continue this motion vigorously and rhythmically, forward and sideward, alternating left over right and right over left. Do not bend elbows.

COUNT:
ONE (arms forward, left over right)
AND (arms sideward)
TWO (arms forward, right over left)
AND (arms sideward) etc.

Repetitions: 10.

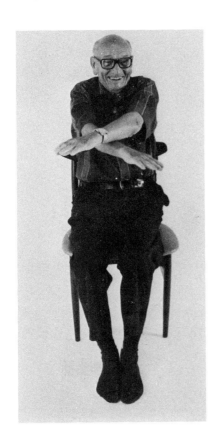

N. Exercises Standing Beside the Chair

1. HAMSTRING FLEXIBILITY

Holding to back of chair, place right heel on chair seat with the leg fully extended. Bend from waist and reach v-e-r-y s-l-o-w-l-y toward calf, ankle, or toes (depending upon beginning flexibility). *Do not bend either knee and do not force any motion.* Bounce very gently to count of 4 and return to standing position.

COUNT:
Bend forward (bouncing very gently to a count of 4)
HOLD 2-3-4
UP
TWO (bend forward) 2-3-4
HOLD 2-3-4
UP etc.

Repetitions: 3 or 4 times on each side

2. FORWARD AND BACKWARD LEG SWINGING
To improve flexibility of hip muscles

Stand erect behind chair, and holding to back, vigorously swing right leg forward and backward, maintaining erect position of upper trunk. Then swing left leg.

COUNT:
ONE (forward)
AND (backward)
TWO (forward)
AND (backward) etc.

Repetitions: 5 minimum, each leg; 10 maximum.

3. SIDE LEG SWINGING

Same position as No. 2.
Swing leg outward to the right, then pull back to starting
position. Reverse position at chair and repeat on
opposite side.

COUNT:
ONE (outward)
AND (back)
TWO (outward)
AND (back) etc.

Repetitions: 5 minimum, each leg; 10 maximum.

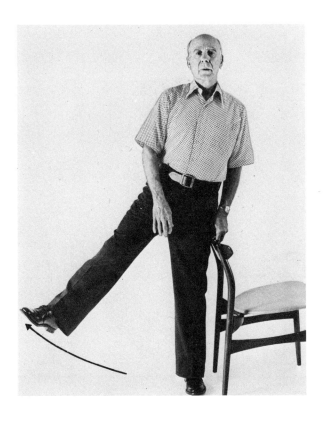

4. PARTIAL KNEE BEND
To strengthen thigh muscles without overstretching the knee joint

Holding back of chair, stand tall and bend the knees halfway down; return to erect position. Remember always to maintain erect position of upper trunk.

COUNT:
ONE (down) *AND* (up)
TWO (down) *AND* (up) etc.

Repetitions: 5.

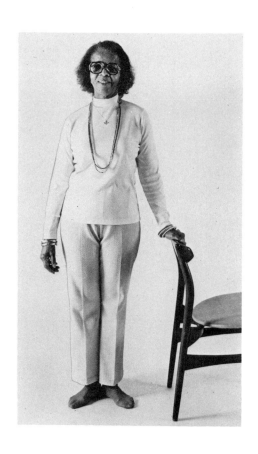

5. KNEE TO CHEST

Standing erect, holding to back of chair, bring right knee upward as far as possible and return. Repeat with left knee.

COUNT:
ONE (up) *AND* (down)
TWO (up) *AND* (down) etc.

Repetitions: 5 each side.

6. CALF MUSCLE EXERCISE
To strengthen the calf muscle and help stimulate flow of blood back toward the heart.

Holding to back of chair, rise up on toes of both feet and back to heels, 15 times.

Then, standing on right foot only, rise up on toes and back to heel 10 times. Repeat on left foot.

COUNT: same as No. 5.

Active older persons should continue with the interval training exercises on page 183.

PART III

Bedside Gymnastics:

For the older person who is confined to bed.

This series is specially designed to improve mood, motivation, and movement and is accepted more responsively with the help of soft background music and the mutual exchange of smiles, repeated from time to time.

Tolerance and the desire of people to perform ''on their own'' will build up quickly if the feeling that someone cares is sincerely conveyed.

We recommend that these exercises be done once a day, five days a week, and in the sequence presented. The exercises should be done to a slow, rhythmic count.

All the exercises in this section should be performed at least once, increasing repetitions by one each week until the maximum number indicated in the text is reached.

Time: 35 to 45 minutes.

A WORD TO THE FRAIL OLDER PERSON

The frail elderly have within themselves the capacity to sit tall, to stand tall, to walk tall, and—especially—to think tall.

Each time you make an effort to be more active, to be a more independent person, you will be taking an important step that not only enhances your own self-image but enhances you in the eyes of those around you.

A. Neck Exercises

To improve function and range of motion of the muscles and joints of neck and upper spine

1. RAISING HEAD

Raise head as far as possible from pillow. Then lower head to resting position.

COUNT:
ONE (up) *AND* (down)
TWO (up) *AND* (down) etc.

Repetitions: 1 or 2 in the beginning. Add 1 repetition each week until you reach a maximum of 10.

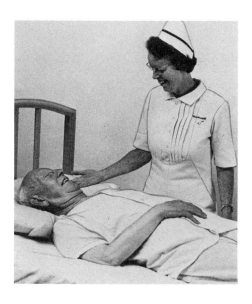
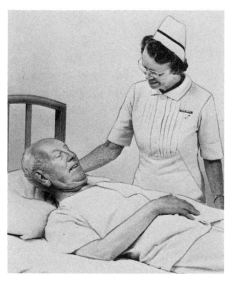

2. TURNING HEAD

Turn head s-l-o-w-l-y to right, then to left.

COUNT: same as No. 1.

Repetitions: 1 or 2 the first week; then add 1 repetition each week until you reach a maximum of 10.

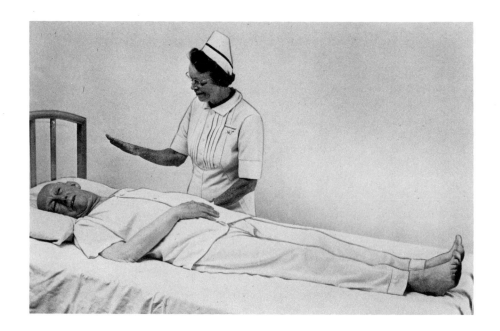

B. Shoulder Exercises

To enhance and improve range of motion in the shoulders

1. SHOULDER SHRUGS

Lying on your back, with your head on the pillow, very slowly shrug your shoulders up and back toward your ears as far as possible.

COUNT:
ONE (shoulders up, toward ears)
AND (down—relax the shoulders)
TWO (up)
AND (down) etc.

Repetitions: 1 or 2 the first week. Add 1 repetition each week until you build to a maximum of 10.

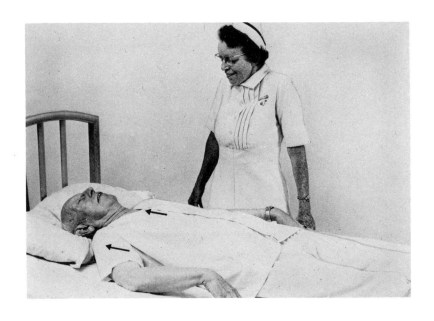

2. SHOULDER ROTATION

Slowly shrug your shoulders up toward your ears, then rotate them forward, down, back, and around. Repeat 5 times. Then do the same exercise five times in the reverse direction: shrug your shoulders up toward your ears, then move them back, down, forward, and around.

COUNT (slowly):
ONE (rotate forward)
AND (completion of rotation)
TWO (forward)
AND (completion of rotation) etc.

Repetitions: 5 times in each direction.

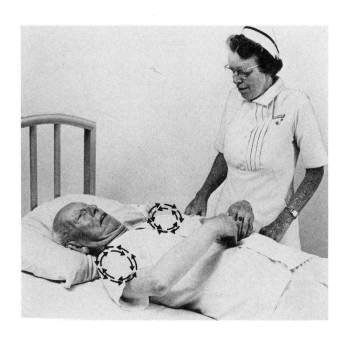

C. Arm Exercises

To improve range of motion in shoulder area

1. ALTERNATE ARM EXTENSION

Lying on your back, raise your right arm straight above your head, close to your ear, while keeping your left arm straight by your side, palm facing down. Now reverse the position of your arms, bringing the right arm to your side and at the same time raising the left arm and extending it over your head.

COUNT:
ONE (right arm over head, left arm to side)
AND (left arm over head, right arm to side)
TWO (right arm over head, left arm to side)
AND (left arm over head, right arm to side) etc.

Repetitions: 5 minimum; 10 maximum.

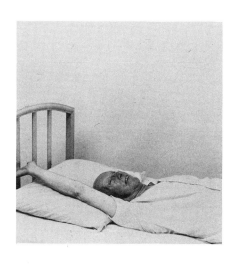 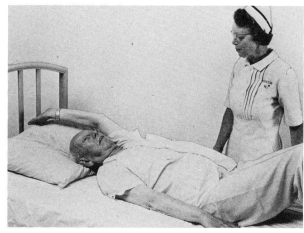

2. ARM CIRCLES

Start with arms fully extended and wrists crossed over abdomen, as shown. Now raise both arms above your head and continue circling in opposite directions. Then circle both arms in the reverse direction.

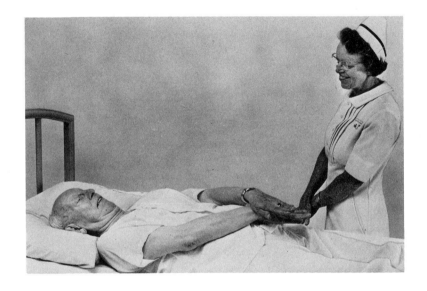

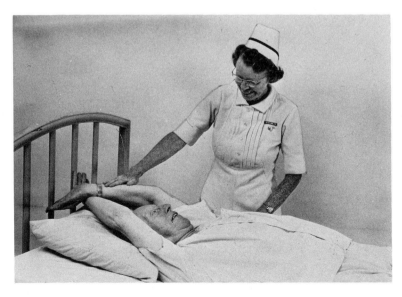

COUNT:
ONE (wrists crossed over abdomen)
AND (wrists crossed above head)
TWO (wrists over abdomen)
AND (wrists above head) etc.

Repetitions: 10.

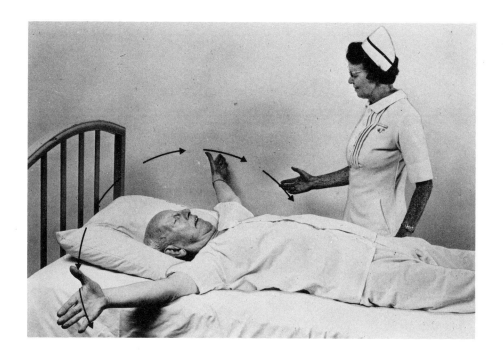

D. Finger and Thumb Exercises

To improve flexibility and circulation; often improves arthritis in fingers and thumbs

1. FINGER FLEXION AND EXTENSION

Holding arms straight and slightly raised, clench fists tightly; then extend fingers slowly.

COUNT:
ONE (clench) *AND* (extend)
TWO (clench) *AND* (extend) etc.

Repetitions: 10.

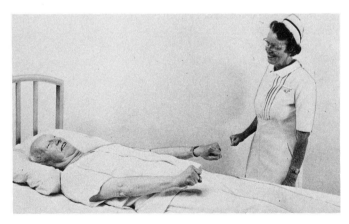

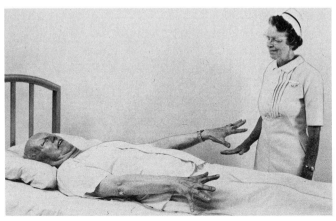

2. FINGER SPREADING

With arms extended forward, spread fingers wide apart and then bring them together.

COUNT:
ONE (apart) *AND* (together)
TWO (apart) *AND* (together) etc.

Repetitions: 10.

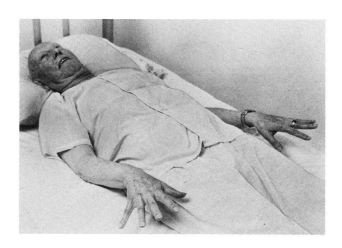

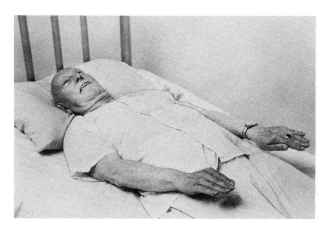

3. THUMB ROTATIONS

Slowly rotate thumbs forward and then in the opposite direction.

COUNT (slowly):
ONE (forward)
AND (completion of rotation)
TWO (forward)
AND (completion of rotation) etc.

Repetitions: 10, each direction.

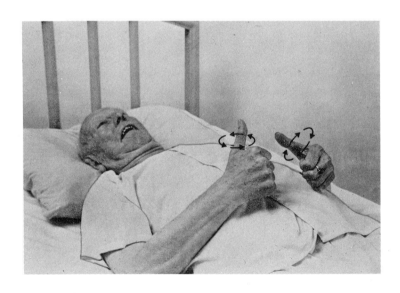

E. Leg Raising

To stretch and improve flexibility of the hamstring muscles behind the knee

Raise your right leg, fully extended, up as far as possible and return. Then do the same exercise with your left leg.

COUNT:
ONE (up) *AND* (down)
TWO (up) *AND* (down) etc.

Repetitions: 10 for each leg.

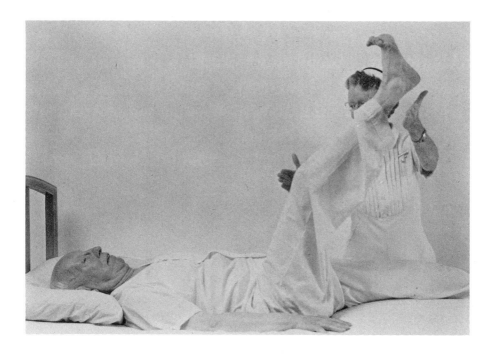

F. Back-relaxing Exercises

To relax the muscles of the lower back and reduce stiffness and tension in that area

1. ONE KNEE TO CHEST

Start from back-lying position, legs straight, arms at sides; grasping right knee with both hands, s-l-o-w-l-y pull knee toward chest, *then* bend head toward knee. Return to starting position.

COUNT:
ONE (right knee toward chest, head toward knee)
AND (starting position, head and leg down)
TWO (right knee toward chest)
AND (starting position)

Repetitions: 5 with each leg.

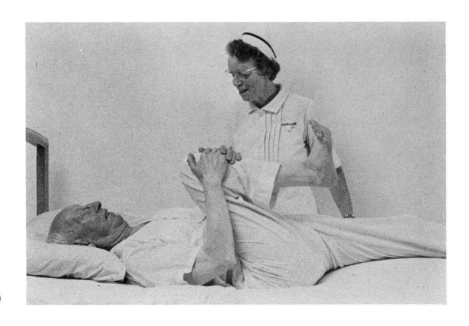

2. BOTH KNEES TOGETHER

Perform exercise No. 1 using both knees at the same time.

COUNT: same as No. 1.

Repetitions: 10.

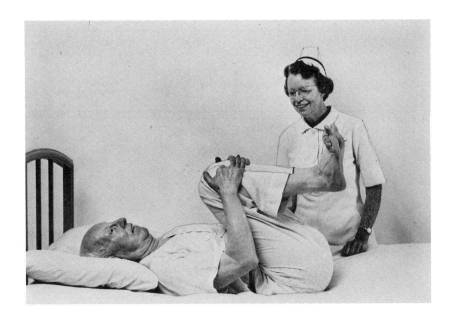

G. Abdominal Exercise

To strengthen the upper and lower abdominal muscles

With arms resting at sides, raise head and shoulders and simultaneously lift both legs up 4 to 6 inches; hold this position for one or two seconds; then relax. Remember to exhale with the effort and inhale as your muscles relax during this exercise.

COUNT:
Exhale *UP*–HOLD–*RELAX*
        TWO–HOLD–*RELAX* etc.

Repetitions: 3 or 4.

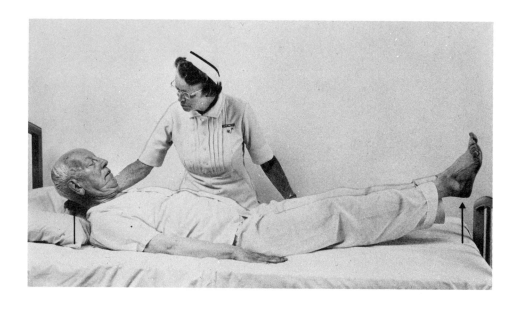

H. Ankle Exercise

To improve range of motion and flexibility in the ankle joint

Extend both ankles slowly as far as possible, then bend them toward shin.

COUNT:
ONE (extend) *AND* (flex toward shin)
TWO (extend) *AND* (flex) etc.

Repetitions: 10.

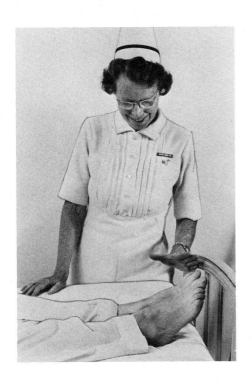 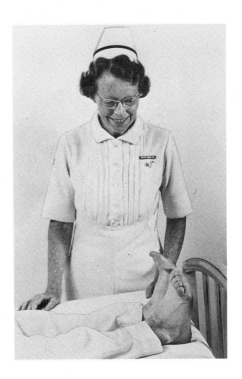

I. Bicycling
To improve abdominal strength and range of motion in the hips

From supine position, bicycle both legs s-l-o-w-l-y.

Repetitions: As many as possible, up to 10.

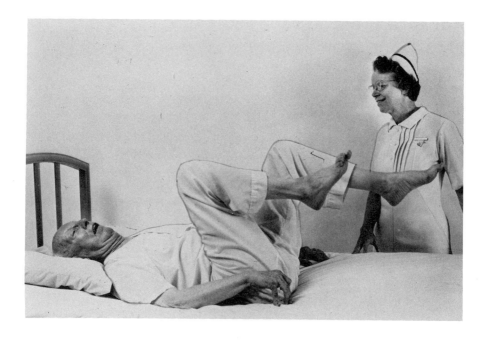

J. Leg Raising from Side-lying Position

To strengthen and improve flexibility of the thighs, hips, and side-of-waist muscles

Lying on right side, raise left leg as high as possible, then return. Repeat, lying on left side and raising right leg.

COUNT:
ONE (up) *AND* (down)
TWO (up) *AND* (down) etc.

Repetitions: 10 each side.

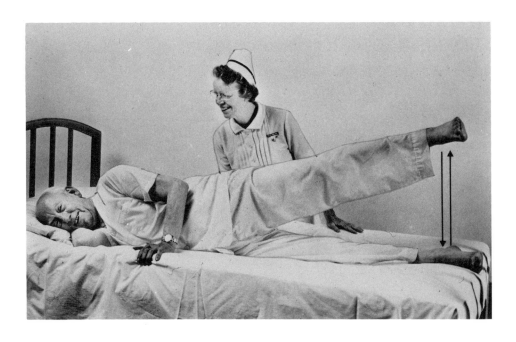

K. Gluteal Exercise
To improve circulation in the
rectal sphincter

IMPORTANT: *Remember to exhale as you tighten the muscles and inhale as you relax them.*

From prone position, chin resting on hands, heels apart, toes together, squeeze gluteal (buttock) muscles tightly together to a s-l-o-w count of four, bringing the heels together. Hold for a count of four, and relax.

COUNT:
ONE-2-3-4 (heels together);
HOLD-2-3-4; RELAX (heels apart)
TWO-2-3-4 (heels together);
HOLD-2-3-4; RELAX (heels apart) etc.

Repetitions: 5

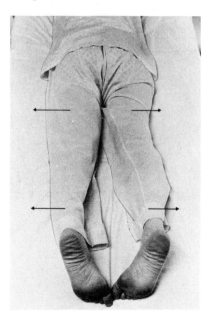 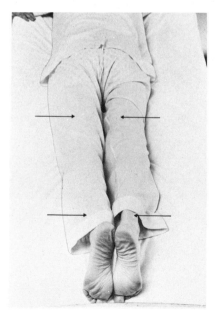

L. Towel Exercises

To strengthen muscles of the arms, shoulders, abdomen, and upper thighs

1. TOWEL CLIMBING

IMPORTANT: *Remember to exhale when you are exerting yourself and inhale when relaxing.*

Very s-l-o-w-l-y pull yourself up almost to a sitting position by grasping towel held by assistant, climbing

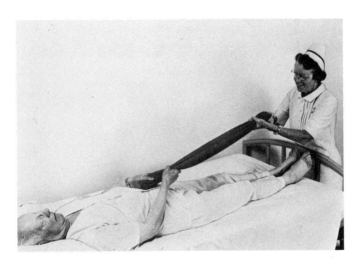

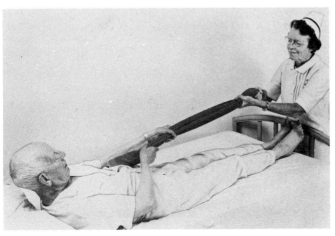

hand over hand; then, just as s-l-o-w-l-y, return to the lying position.

COUNT:
UP-2-3-4 DOWN-2-3-4; RELAX
TWO-2-3-4 DOWN-2-3-4; RELAX

Repetitions: 3.

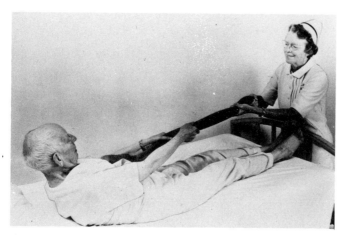

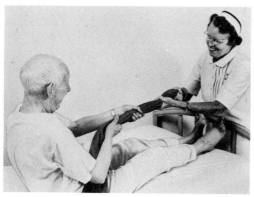
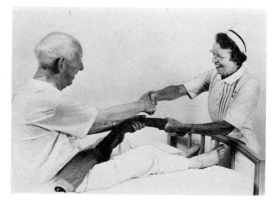

2. TOWEL PULL-UP

Gripping towel held by assistant, as illustrated, s-l-o-w-l-y pull yourself to a near sitting position; then s-l-o-w-l-y return to lying position.

COUNT (slowly):
UP-2-3-4 DOWN-2-3-4; RELAX
TWO-2-3-4 DOWN-2-3-4; RELAX

Repetitions: 3.

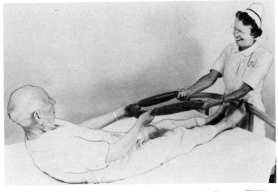

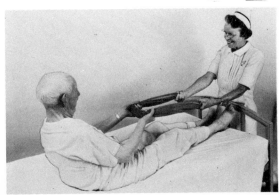

3. QUADRICEP EXERCISE
To strengthen thigh muscles which help support the weight of the entire body.

With assistant holding towel under the ankles to elevate legs about 15 inches, lower legs back to the bed slowly, against the resistance of the towel.

COUNT: LEGS UP
                  DOWN-2-3-4
                  LEGS UP
                  DOWN-2-3-4 etc.

Repetitions: 3.

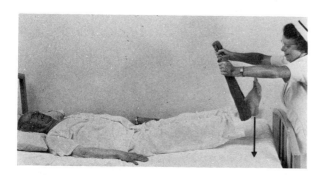

4. TOWEL RAISING TO SHOULDER HEIGHT
This towel exercise and the two that follow will increase strength and mobility of the shoulders.

Sitting on side of bed and holding towel at shoulder width, extend arms and rest hands on thighs; pull towel taut. Raise towel to shoulder height, still exerting lateral pull with both hands; return to thighs.

COUNT:
ONE (up) *AND* (down)
TWO (up) *AND* (down) etc.

Repetitions: 10.

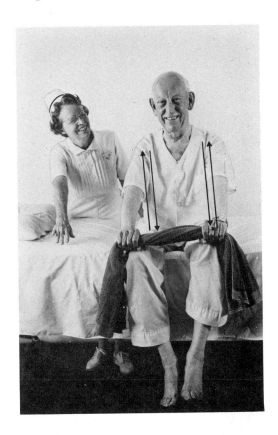

5. TOWEL RAISING ABOVE HEAD

From same position as No. 4, raise towel up and over head, reaching toward the ceiling, and then down to thighs. Remember to keep your arms at shoulder width and hold the towel taut.

COUNT: Same as No. 4.

Repetitions: 10.

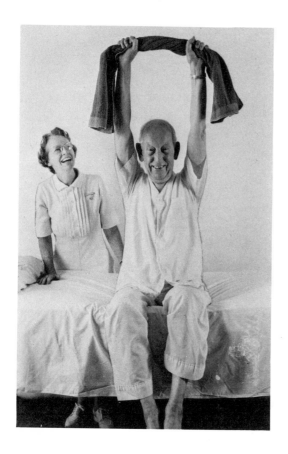

6. TOWEL HOLDING BEHIND NECK

From same starting position as No. 4, with arms at shoulder width, bring towel forward, up, and behind the neck in one motion; return to thighs. Hold your head erect and do not drop your chin; try not to force this exercise.

COUNT: Same as No. 4.

Repetitions: 5.

7. TOWEL TWISTS

Holding the towel taut behind neck, arms at shoulder width, and the elbows down, twist upper body from waist—alternately right to left.

COUNT:
ONE (twist to the right)
AND (twist to the left)
TWO (right)
AND (left) etc.

Repetitions: 5.

M. Hip Raising

To strengthen and tone the lower back and abdominal muscles

Raise hips only (arms at side) about 6 inches from the bed; hold this position momentarily, then relax.

COUNT: HIPS UP-HOLD-RELAX
            TWO UP-HOLD-RELAX etc.

Repetitions: 5.

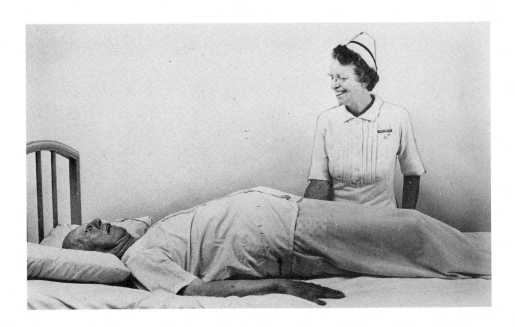

N. Preparation for Walking

1. STRENGTHENING THIGH MUSCLES

Holding the wrists of an assistant, stand up on stepstool slowly, then sit down *very slowly*. As you bend your legs and s-l-o-w-l-y lower yourself to the edge of the bed, count one-thousand-and-ONE, one-thousand-and-TWO, etc., for a period of about six counts.

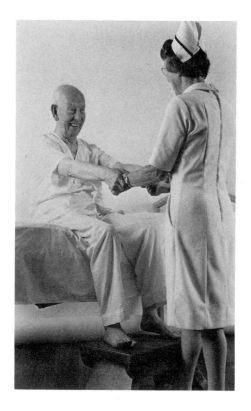
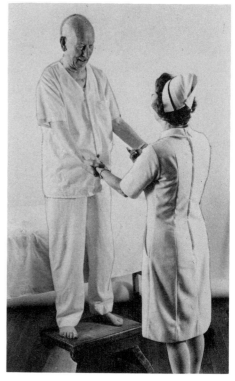

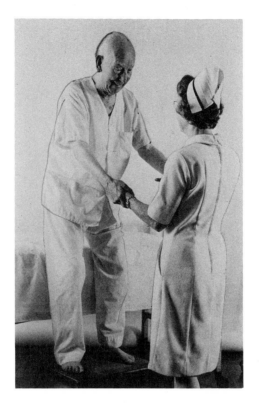

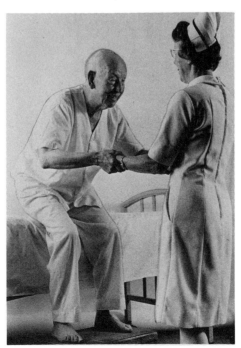

2. STRENGTHENING CALF MUSCLES

Holding assistant's wrists with both hands, rise up and down on your toes, keeping your body erect; do not lean forward.

COUNT:
ONE (up) *AND* (down)
TWO (up) *AND* (down) etc.

Repetitions: 10.

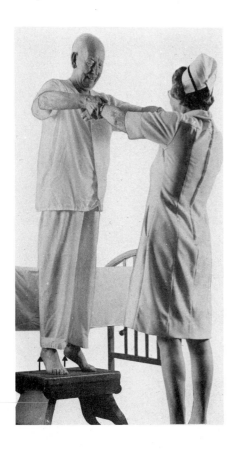

O. Walking

With help, step down from stool and walk forward a few steps, turn around, walk back to bed, step up on stool, turn around, and sit down on bed.

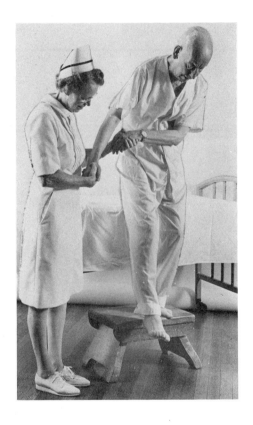

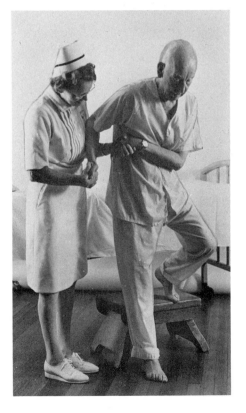

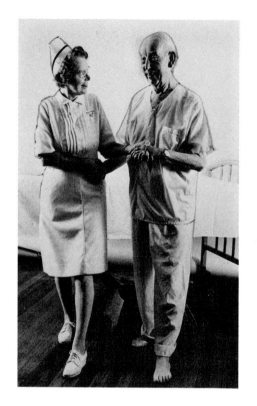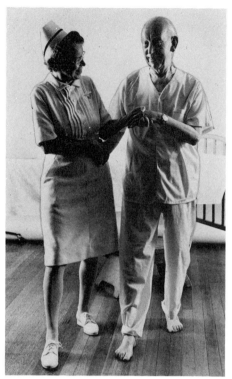

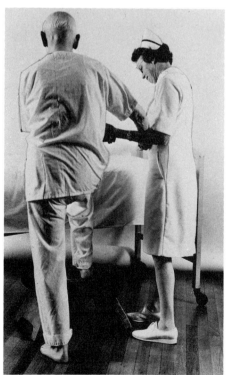

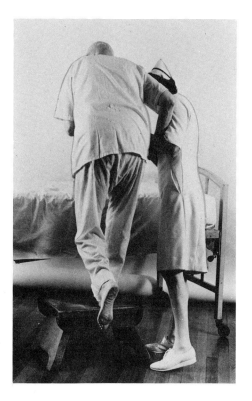

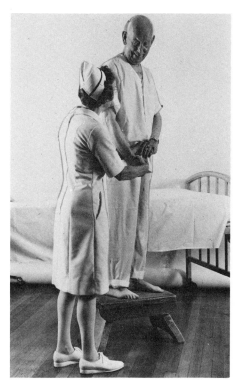

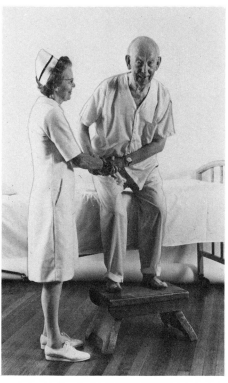

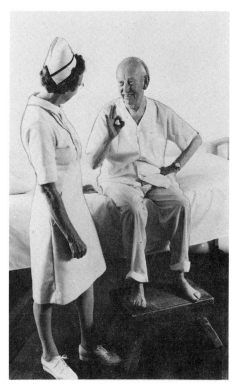

PART IV

Interval Training Exercises for Endurance:

The concluding part of the exercise session for active older persons who have performed the exercises in Part I or Part II.

These interval training exercises are designed to build your endurance and strengthen your heart and lungs without causing fatigue. They should be performed to a rhythmic count with a reasonably lively cadence.

Before engaging in endurance-type exercises, be sure that your physician approves.

Introduction

Interval training is a method of building endurance—strengthening the heart and lungs—that is particularly adaptable for the older person because it builds endurance with a minimum of fatigue.

Each interval of an endurance-type exercise should be *no longer* than one minute, followed by an equal amount of time idling (that is, walking about slowly).

We recommend that you begin these exercises with *three* intervals, alternated with *three* periods of *idling*. Under no circumstances should your heart rate exceed 120 beats per minute.

If in any single interval the heart rate is accelerated beyond this recommended target, *cut down the duration* of the interval by one quarter or one half.

Most older persons, after training, will be able to build their tolerance from the initial 3 intervals to an optimum of 10.

Be sure to regularly check your heart rate.

We recommend that immediately after stopping the exercise you count the number of heartbeats for 6 seconds, then add a zero. (This will give you the correct heart rate per minute, which means multiplying the number of beats by 10.)

If you have counted 8 heartbeats in 6 seconds, your heart rate per minute will be 80. If you have counted 10 beats in 6 seconds your heart rate per minute will be 100, and so forth.

SUGGESTIONS FOR TAKING HEART RATE

Every individual should learn how to take his or her *resting* heart rate *and* the heart rate *immediately* after *exercise*.

Take either the radial pulse, at wrist, or the carotid pulse, in the neck.

Taking radial pulse

Taking carotid pulse

TAKING YOUR OWN PULSE REQUIRES ONLY A WATCH OR A CLOCK WITH A SWEEP SECOND HAND.

RESTING HEART RATE

The resting heart rate should be taken for 15 seconds, then multiply the number of beats by 4. This will ascertain your resting heart rate per minute. If your *resting* heart rate is above 100, we suggest that you consult with your physician and get his approval *before* you begin these or any vigorous exercises.

IMMEDIATE HEART RATE

Immediate heart rate should be taken the instant you stop or pause in any endurance exercise or activity.

To calculate your immediate heart rate, count the number of times your heart beats in 6 seconds, then multiply by 10. (As mentioned before, this is done by adding a zero to the number of heartbeats counted.)

TARGET HEART RATE

There is a direct relationship between age and the highest heart rate you are able to attain through exercise. As your age increases, your maximum heart rate decreases. Therefore, in designing an exercise program for older individuals, we have used the concept of a *target heart rate*, based on 80 percent of maximal heart rate, which sets a safe limit for achieving fitness while keeping stress and fatigue to a minimum.

The following chart of target heart rates will help you to determine the amount of exercise that is sufficient to condition your cardiovascular system without overexerting yourself.

We recommend, as a general rule, that older persons, especially those who are over 70 or who have not exercised before, limit their heart rates to between 110–115 beats per minute. However, if you are normally active and in good general health, you can feel reasonably safe if you stay within the target zone on the following page, allowing yourself 5 points more or less from the suggested rates.

TARGET HEART RATES (THR)*
Based on 80% of Maximal Heart Rate

AGE	THR	AGE	THR	AGE	THR	AGE	THR	AGE	THR
20	160	30	152	40	144	50	136	60	128
21	159	31	151	41	143	51	135	61	127
22	158	32	150	42	142	52	134	62	126
23	158	33	150	43	142	53	134	63	126
24	157	34	149	44	141	54	133	64	125
25	156	35	148	45	140	55	132	65	124
26	155	36	147	46	139	56	131	66	123
27	154	37	146	47	138	57	130	67	122
28	154	38	146	48	138	58	130	68	122
29	153	39	145	49	137	59	129	69	121

*If you have not exercised before or are over 70, do not exceed 110–115 heart beats per minute.

Straddle Exercises

To build endurance and improve agility, balance, and coordination of muscles of the lower trunk and extremities*

1. FLOOR STRADDLE

Starting position: hands on hips, legs together.

a. Jump to *straddle* (legs apart) and return to starting position; repeat 5 times.

b. Jump to *stride* position (legs alternating, forward and backward); repeat 5 times.

c. *Run in place*, bringing knees up as far as possible (not illustrated); repeat 5 times.

*The straddle exercise can be done either standing alone or holding onto a chair. After doing this exercise, you may proceed to another interval exercise of your choice.

d. *Hop* on *both feet* to a height of about 4 inches; repeat 5 times.

e. *Hop alternately* on *right* and *left* foot. 5 times on each foot.

Combine all movements in one interval (a,b,c,d,e), rhythmically and continually, 5 repetitions each; this will take approximately 15 seconds. Take your immediate heart rate and slowly walk about until resting heart rate has returned to 100 or below, then resume next interval.

In the beginning, do no more than 3 intervals, adding one interval each week. Ten intervals is the optimum goal, with your heart rate never accelerating beyond 110–115 beats per minute.

2. CHAIR STRADDLE

Starting position: holding to back of chair, legs together.

a. Jump to *straddle* (legs apart) and return to starting position; repeat 5 times.
b. Jump to *stride* position (legs alternating, forward and backward); repeat 5 times.
c. *Run in place,* bringing knees up as far as possible; repeat 5 times.
d. *Hop on both feet* to a height of about 4 inches; repeat 5 times.
e. *Hop alternately* on *right* and *left* foot, 5 times on each foot.

Combine all movements in one interval rhythmically and continually, 5 repetitions each; this will take approximately 15 seconds. Take immediate heart rate and relax until resting heart rate has returned to 100 or below, then resume next interval.

In the beginning, do no more than 3 intervals, adding one interval each week. Ten intervals is the optimum goal, with your heart rate never accelerating beyond 110–115 beats per minute.

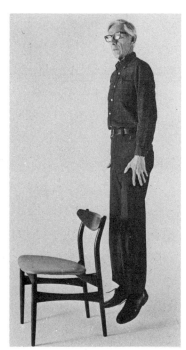

Step Bench Exercise

You will need a 10- to 12-inch sturdy step bench or stool, constructed so it will not tip over.

Step up with left foot to erect position on bench; then step down with left foot to resume erect position on floor.

COUNT: *Step*-up-step-down
           Two-up-step-down
           Three-up-step-down etc.
           (20 maximum per minute)

Using the cadence of 20 steps per minute, and watching a sweep second hand, perform the exercise for one minute—leading with the left foot. Take immediate heart rate, then walk slowly about until the heart rate returns to 100 beats per minute or less.

Continue exercise, leading with the right foot.

Three intervals are suggested for beginners, adding 1 each week until the optimum of 10 is achieved. Be sure to check that your heart rate at no time exceeds 110–115 beats per minute.

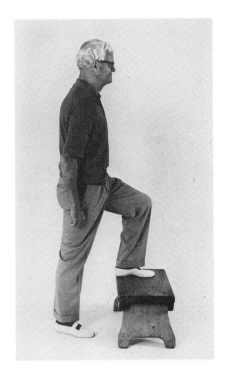 

Step (left foot on bench) Up (both feet on bench)

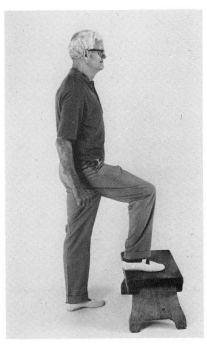 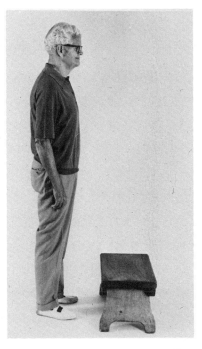

Step (left foot on floor) Down (both feet on floor) **193**

Alley Cat Routine

We have adopted the Alley Cat routine for our interval exercises because its rhythm and cadence very seldom accelerate the heart rate beyond 110–115 beats per minute. The dance movements may be performed from standing position or from a chair or wheelchair.

For musical background, we use Lawrence Welk's unique arrangement of Alley Cat, which we have found is not only an excellent accompaniment for interval training but also adds to your *joie de vivre* while exercising.

The Alley Cat recording is from Lawrence Welk's Ranwood Records (RLP 8005), titled *Myron Floren's New Sound*.

1. Standing tall with weight on left foot (or sitting erect in chair), move right foot to the right side and back, two times to a count of *ONE-AND-TWO-AND*.

2. When the right foot comes back on the *AND* count the second time, *IMMEDIATELY* put your weight on the right foot and move the left foot to the left side and back, two times to count of *THREE-AND-FOUR-AND*.

3. When the left foot comes back on the *AND* count, move the right foot *backward* and *forward*, two times to a count of *ONE-AND-TWO-AND*.

4. Repeat with left foot, moving backward and forward, two times to a count of *THREE-AND-FOUR-AND*.

5. Now bring the right knee up as far as possible, two times to a count of *ONE-AND-TWO-AND*.

6. Bring the left knee up and down, two times to a count of *THREE-AND-FOUR-AND*.

7. Raise the right knee up and slap it with your right hand.

8. Raise the left knee up and slap it with your left hand.

9. Clap your hands and make one quarter turn to the right.

10. You are now ready to start another cycle if your heart rate is no more than 110–115 beats per minute.

Remember that these are short, quick steps. Changing weight from one foot to the other quickly is important so that you can keep in step with the music.

As with the other heart-strengthening exercises in this section, limit each interval to 1 minute followed by 1 minute of idling or walking about. Begin with 3 intervals, adding one each week until the maximum of 10 is reached.

Rope Skipping

Persons over sixty years of age should skip rope only after they have consulted their physician. For those who are able, rope skipping is an excellent cardiovascular skill and endurance-builder. It provides the same physical benefits for your body as jogging but is superior for older persons because it can be done any time of the year regardless of the weather and requires only a few feet of clothesline. Rope skipping is an ideal form of exercise because it allows you to expend the greatest amount of energy in the smallest space.

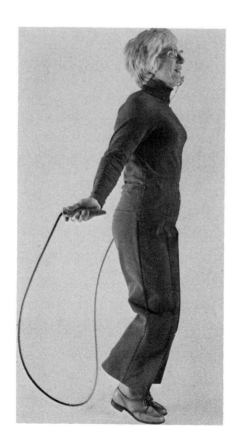

You can skip rope indoors or out on a variety of surfaces, including grass, hard rubber mats such as gymnasium mats, carpeted floors, and so forth. Avoid skipping rope on any hard, unyielding surface—for example, a concrete or hardwood floor—and always be sure to wear proper footwear, such as tennis shoes or sturdy rubber-soled shoes.

It is important that your rope be the proper length and heavy enough to maintain an even speed. We recommend a No. 9 sash cord (or 9/32 inch in diameter), which can be found in most hardware stores. To measure the proper length, stand with both feet on the center of the rope—the rope should then be long enough to reach from armpit to armpit.

Music enhances mood, motivation, and movement and should be selected according to your individual performance and preference. Musical selections for the more lively steps include Herb Alpert's Tijuana Brass album, *Whipped Cream and Other Delights*, A & M Records (LP110, SP4110) and André Kostelanetz, *Concert in the Park*, Columbia Records CS9488.

The intervals should consist of skipping for 1 minute, followed by idling (walking around) for 1 minute. Depending on your heart rate, begin with 3 intervals. Add 1 interval each week until you reach the maximum of 10. Check your heart rate after each minute of skipping to be sure you are not exceeding 110–115 beats per minute.

PART V

Exercises for Special Problems

The following supplementary exercises will improve dexterity and strength in your fingers and hands and help your balance and coordination.

These exercises should be performed in addition to your regular exercise program as needed.

Let Your Fingers Do the Walking

To develop strength, dexterity, and suppleness of the fingers

Using a 24-inch section of broomstick, with only the *first joint of thumb and fingers* of right hand, start at top of broomstick and, *maintaining* its *vertical position throughout,* travel s-l-o-w-l-y down to the bottom. Alternate hands for several repetitions.

The Balance Beam
To enhance balance and coordination

The stereotype of the aged individual—stooped and shuffling in gait, uncoordinated and slow of mind—can be attributed somewhat to the apprehension and fear of falling older people often have. In our experience, the following exercise produces a dramatic improvement—renewed confidence, more graceful carriage, and improved mobility—in a very few weeks' time.

You will need a 2-inch-wide smooth wooden beam, 10 or 12 feet long, shaped like a railroad track. (This is the standard beam used in schools throughout the country.) The beam should not be more than 3 to 4 inches above the floor.

IMPORTANT: *Balance beam exercises are recommended only in a group setting where trained supervision is available. The instructor should constantly "spot" each participant with a helping hand.*

1. Walk forward the length of the balance beam, standing tall and concentrating on good posture. Do not bend at the waist. Use a good walking stride, with each step about 8 or 10 inches.

2. When you have mastered this, try walking backward, as illustrated.

3. Walk forward a few steps, take a slightly longer stride, and try to balance yourself as you drop to your knee.

Combine all three movements, by walking forward, dropping to the knee every few steps, and then walking backward.

Repetitions: Move up and down the length of the balance beam several times.

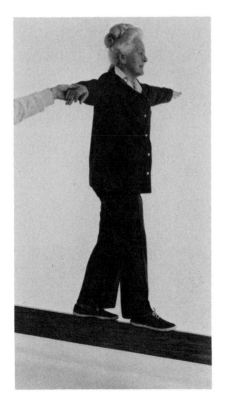 

Grip and Finger Exercise
To help inhibit arthritis and the joint degeneration in hands and fingers

There is a demonstrated correlation between your total strength and the strength of your grip.

Grasp a normal-sized newspaper page, 17 by 21 inches, in the center with the *first joint of thumb and fingers* of your left hand, palm facing down. With your palm still facing downward and using only the first finger joints of one hand, gradually crumple the newspaper sheet until the paper is pressed into a small ball shape. Repeat with fresh page of newspaper for right hand.

This exercise is a fairly vigorous one, but we have found that, with practice, it will do much to ameliorate the loss of function and strength in the fingers that many older people experience.

PART VI

Exercises for Relaxation and Peace of Mind

*Try to set aside a few moments each day "just to relax."
You will find these special exercises can help you
release tension and achieve a feeling of tranquility and
serenity.*

Medicine Ball

There are few among us who have not at times felt the urge to lash out, to kick, to punch someone, or by invective to rid ourselves of the pent-up anger, passion, hostility, and other frustrations that build up in daily life. Older persons who are lonely, bitter, or depressed often experience relief and some exhilaration from the following simple exercise.

Toss a six-pound medicine ball to a stolid receiver. Repeat a half dozen times or more. This is a simple tool we strongly recommend. The therapeutic effect is almost immediately observable.

A Technique for Relaxation and Serenity

The position illustrated, called hook lying, is one of complete relaxation and is very useful in helping you slow down if you feel tense. You can use a 15-inch bench, as pictured, or substitute a couch, chair, or stool.

Place your buttocks as close as possible to the base of the bench; rest your legs, from the knees down, on top of the bench. Your head should be resting comfortably on a folded towel and your back should be perfectly flat against the floor. Fold your hands and place them on your abdomen. There is no pull of gravity on your pelvic area when you are in this position, hence the feeling of total bodily relaxation.

Breathe very quietly, *with no effort to inhale deeply*. This encourages a slight up and down movement of the diaphragm against the weight of your hands. After you have established a pattern of breathing in this way (after about a minute or so), take a *very slightly* deeper breath so that your diaphragm rises as you inhale and hold the breath for one or two seconds; then, through pursed lips, exhale as slowly as possible; as you exhale, your diaphragm will slowly go down. With practice, you should be able to take as long as 15 seconds to fully exhale.

To repeat: As you breathe in, your abdomen comes up; as you exhale slowly, it relaxes downward.

This exercise should be performed for at least 3 to 5 minutes.

PART VII

Reflections

Tranquility
Hate Not, Anger Not, Envy Not
A Sound Mind in a Sound Body

A Sad Refrain

The saddest refrain may be that of an ache or pain. It is one complaint to which no one cares to listen. The German philosopher Schopenhauer remarked that the two foes to human happiness are pain and boredom.

Why are the mass of elderly Americans (with few exceptions) such classical bores? They often dislike the company of those their own age. We have often heard octogenarians exclaim, ''I can't stand being around old people.''

It is sadly true that many of them are not interesting, and are interested in very little.

There were times when grandparents were exciting and stimulating to their children and to their grandchildren—they had skills and wisdom to share—but today's world leaves many older people sadly behind, segregated from the mainstream of life, away and apart from those only a generation younger, unable to share their heritage, that of dispensing their wisdom, happily and unselfishly.

America cannot boast about the quality of life it has made possible for its senior citizens. Yet senior citizens need not harbor these indignities, if, instead, they attempt to nurture their own self-respect.

Accept not the role of a child with games and crafts and being led by the hand.

Be interested and hence interesting; eschew the talk of minor ills and pains, for no one really cares—be up and about as actively as your limbs permit; a bit more and more each day. A new world will reward your efforts, a smiling countenance replace a frown. And you will have accomplished this on your very own!

Vignette

It is refreshing to meet a young person in whom there is something of the old, but more so to find an old person with the spirit of the young. Those who follow this maxim may in time have the appearance of age, but never be anything but young in mind and heart.

Although described differently, this feeling was strongly expressed by Cicero in his *de Senectute*. We see this admirable trait in many of the men and women who have participated in our exercise programs. They are the truly elite among their own contemporaries, constantly radiating warmth and charm—a joy to be with.

We recall a vivacious lady in her ninth decade who remarked to us, ''Mr. Frankel, don't you think at my age it is rather late in life to start an exercise program?''

I replied rather facetiously, ''Remember, Sarah in the Bible conceived and was delivered of a child after she was 90.'' Her quick and smiling retort was, ''Find me a good man and I might try to emulate Sarah.''

If there is a ''magic'' way for our older citizens to assure their perennial youthfulness, it is to habitually and actively stimulate both mind and body.

"Fitness is ageless . . . and forever young at heart"

C.T. resided in one of Charleston, West Virginia's newly built, high-rise, senior-citizen residence units—comfortably ensconced in a small, well-appointed apartment. Suddenly sickness and a multiplicity of medical problems confined her to her bed, necessitating the help of neighbors to feed, bathe, cook, and carry a bedpan every day.

A local attorney who became interested in C.T.'s problems asked us if we could help her avoid the alternative of a nursing care facility. There were neither family nor funds to lighten the burden. Administrators of the residence center, as gently as possible, told her of their inability to care for anyone in her condition.

Intrigued by the challenge, we called upon C.T. and offered a planned exercise regime, to be done several times daily—demanding only strict compliance, subject to her physician's restrictions.

With desperation as the catalyst, C.T. was out of her bed and walking laboriously but alone within two weeks, bypassing at our insistence both wheelchair and walker.

C.T., 75, now joins our active exercise group three times weekly, participating in rhythmic calisthenics, posture exercises, and some lively dance routines: alert, smiling, happy to be once again in the mainstream of life.

Dozens of similar case histories suggest that carefully planned programs of fitness for older persons are not only viable but far preferable alternatives to dependency in later years.

Movement—Mind and Aging!

Dr. Hans Kreitler and his wife, of the Tel Aviv University Department of Psychology, conducted a study on Movement and Aging in which they compared the joy with which children and young people engage in motion for the sake of motion with the reluctance to be physically active that sedentary adults tend to feel more and more as they advance in years.*

The Kreitlers found that adults who led inactive lives experienced not only increased muscular deterioration as they grew older but also experienced distinct changes in their mental processes.

Older people who are habitually inactive gradually lose confidence in their physical abilities and come to view themselves as weak or uncoordinated or clumsy. And this distorted perception of themselves and their bodies very often becomes the reality: They *do* become clumsy or awkward and, as time goes on, develop a real fear of any physical activity at all! Since their physical energy has no outlet, they turn their feelings of frustration inwardly against themselves and suffer depression, insomnia, and fretfulness.

Regular bodily exercise is the best way to release this pent-up energy. Physical activity can provide deep emotional satisfaction and restore a positive self-image.

*Kreitler, H., and Kreitler, S.: "Movement and Aging: A Psychological Approach." *Medicine and Sport,* Vol. 4: *Physical Activity and Aging,* pp. 302–6 (Basel: Karger, 1970).

The Joy of Walking

Walking is one of the simplest, most basic physical activities, and it is also one of the most beneficial. It enables you to commune with nature, with a chosen companion or with your personal deity! You may trod the soft earth, stopping to smell the flowers, observe the changing hues of the foliage, hearken to the songs of the creatures of the woods—or, in contrast, be similarly uplifted as you make your way through the streets of a metropolitan city, strolling by mini-parks and along crowded thoroughfares, enjoying the cacophony of the big city and the charm of the colorful and varied window displays.

No matter where you do it, walking has a tonic effect on mind, spirit, and body. We encourage you to pursue this healthful activity as often as you can. Consider this fact: If you simply walk for an hour or more, frequently changing pace, your blood will be effectively squeezed upward through the valves in the veins of the lower extremities and back toward the heart, enriching your entire circulatory system with oxygen and other nutrients, enhancing respiration, and tranquilizing the most jaded spirit.

We should not and must not neglect to add this important exercise to our activity armamentarium!

On Your Rocker

As we progress from infancy to childhood, we gradually outgrow the need for cradle-rocking and breast or bottle feeding without much aftereffect. And as we pass on to early adolescence, we leave behind us with nary a thought an assortment of habits, such as thumb-sucking or clinging to a favorite ''security'' blanket, that have been stalwart childhood companions.

For most of us, however, regardless of our age, the rocking chair remains a perennial favorite, a popular and much-enjoyed piece of furniture whose soothing rhythmic motion never fails to gently lull us to a feeling of quiet and calm, no matter how tense or unsettled we may feel when we first begin to rock.

Rocking is not only a soothing activity, it is also beneficial to your health. In his book *Touching*, Dr. Ashley Montagu, who has been a professor at Harvard, New York University, and the University of California, has this to say concerning the *therapeutic* benefits of the rocking chair:

> Rocking chairs are to be highly recommended for adults, and especially the aging. The activity of rocking increases cardiac output (cardiac output is the amount of blood pumped by the heart per minute), it promotes respiration and discourages lung congestion. It stimulates muscle tone and not least important maintains the feeling of relatedness. A general stimulation of the internal organs results from the rocking.

We have found that, simple as it seems, the rocking chair is an excellent tool to help you to relax and at the same time contribute to your general physical well-being. We strongly recommend that you use it instead of sitting in an easy chair or on a couch. You will find that it is not only more comfortable—for your body and your mind—but better for you.

Psychology of Music and Laughter

In Plato's Fourth Book of the Republic, he states, "Now health in body and mind which controls and improves the body, is to be obtained through music and gymnastics, which should continue throughout life—and he who mingles music with gymnastics in the fairest proportions, and best attempers them to the soul, may be called the true harmonist in a far higher sense than the tuner of strings."

The ancient Egyptians called music "physic for the soul" and had much faith in its remedial qualities.

The famous American physiologist Walter Cannon was able to show that music affected the emotions, resulting in release of adrenaline and perhaps other hormones.

It has often been shown that properly chosen music may reduce or delay the onset of fatigue and thus contribute greatly to increasing muscular endurance.

Smiling and laughter are muscular actions and can relax the mind and body, as any physician can testify. They are a more effective tonic than any drug, and they certainly contribute to physiological well-being.

Diet and Nutrition

In his book *Human Nutrition,* Dr. Jean Mayer, formerly a professor at Harvard University, currently president of Tufts University, states, "The consumption of a varied diet, adapted in amount to individual needs; avoidance of dietary excesses, of an excessively fat diet; moderate salt intake; generous fluid intake, and sufficient exercise and rest are as valid for old age as they are for young and middle-age adults."

The word *diet* comes from the Greek *diaita,* meaning way of life. Long before there was a science of nutrition, farmers knew that when they wished fat cattle for market, they closed the pasture gate; and when it was desirable to have lean stock, they opened the gate, giving the animals freedom to roam the range.

If your way of life embraces avoidance of sweets, limitation of animal fats and fried foods, and a sensible intake of low-fat dairy products, a variety of fruits and vegetables, and whole wheat bread, all in reasonably sensible portions and coupled with an equally wise admixture of physical activity, your cup of health should run over.

Fitness Abhors Fatness

Among Americans of all economic levels, obesity is on the increase. As if this were not sufficient cause for alarm, related to the rise in obesity is a growing number of deaths from diseases of the heart and kidney and from diabetes.

Obesity is a serious health problem at any age, but it poses an especially great hazard for older people who may have difficulty in moving about and getting proper exercise and, as a result, are not capable of taking complete care of themselves. In addition, both muscular efficiency and coordination seem to decrease with age, and the added burden of excess weight renders the elderly more prone to falls, accidents, and broken bones and substantially increases their risk should surgery ever be required. Most important of all, excessive weight means a reduction in longevity; very few people who are obese live to a ripe old age.

What can you do to prevent obesity or, if necessary, shed extra pounds?

We recommend that you follow a slow and sensible program of *losing weight* accompanied by *stepped-up physical activity*. Ask your physician to give you a proper diet—one that provides sufficient nutrition but will cut down on fats and salt intake and keep the number of calories you consume each day at a reasonable level. Stay away from so-called "miracle" drugs and crash diets: these are dangerous for young people and even more so for older people, who are often victimized by false advertising claims that promise special nutritional benefits. If you eat normal foods and avoid diet fads, there is seldom any need for extra vitamins, unless they are specifically prescribed by your physician.

Sprinkle each day liberally with sufficient rest and exercise. Varied physical activities are a healthy substitute for the nibbling and snacking that often go along with just plain boredom. If you do the exercises in this book for even half an hour or an hour each day, you will soon begin to tone your body and lose excess pounds. In addition, the exercises will help you to improve such physical difficulties as arthritis. The combination of proper diet and increased physical activity will multiply your positive feelings about yourself and increase your ability to enjoy life as you increase your capacity to move about freely.

Breaking Icons

The phrase ''Senior Citizen'' is a societal stereotype
which is often meant to describe our elders as shuffling
in gait, stooped in posture, and slow of mind. We forget
that most of the problems of the world have been
initiated by the vigorous young and middle-aged—and
that in times of crisis, experienced leaders, like
Germany's Adenauer in his eighties, and the vigorous
but aged Churchill, have been called to restore order
from chaos.

The multimillions over sixty have given to our nation
much more than they can ever receive in return. They
have the valuable knowledge, perception, and wisdom
that can be garnered only from a lifetime of experience
and the richness of feeling that comes only from years of
loving others. They have the right to step out briskly in
well-deserved pride.

Try your body as vigorously as your strength allows,
nurture your mind as steadfastly, and reap the rewards
of the known interrelationship between the physical, the
mental, and the emotional—for fitness is ageless and
forever young at heart.

Bibliography and References

Andersen, K. Lange, et al. *Fundamentals of Exercise Testing*. Geneva: World Health Organization, 1970.

Åstrand, Per-Olof. *Experimental Studies of Physical Working Capacity in Relation to Sex and Age*. Copenhagen: Ejnar Munksgaard, 1952.

—— and Kaare Rodahl. *Textbook of Work Physiology,* 2nd ed. New York: McGraw-Hill, 1977.

Beauvoir, Simone de. *The Coming of Age*. New York: G.P. Putnam's Sons, 1972.

Best, Charles Herbert, and Norman Burke Taylor. *The Physiological Basis of Medical Practice*. Baltimore: Williams and Wilkins Company, 1961.

Bierman, William, and Sidney Licht. *Physical Medicine in General Practice*. New York: Hoeber-Harper, 1959.

Bjerre, Poul. *The History and Practice of Psychoanalysis*. London: The Gorham Press, 1916.

Blackburn, Henry, ed. "Measurement in Exercise Electrocardiography." Papers presented at the Ernst Simonson Conference. Springfield, Ill.: Charles C Thomas Publisher, 1964.

Blakeslee, Alton, and Jeremiah Stamler. *Your Heart Has Nine Lives*. Englewood Cliffs, N.J.: Prentice-Hall, 1963.

Blumenfeld, Arthur. *Heart Attack: Are You a Candidate?* New York: Paul S. Eriksson, 1964.

Blumenthal, Herman T., ed. *Interdisciplinary Topics in Gerontology. Psychological Functioning in the Normal Aging and Senile Aged,* Vol. 1; *Methodological Problems in Cross-National Studies in Aging,* Vol. 2; *Colloquium on Health and Aging of the Population,* Vol. 3;

Decision Making and Age, Vol. 4; *Research Training and Practice in Clinical Medicine of Aging,* Vol. 5. Basel: S. Karger, 1968–70.

Bowen, Wilbur Pardon. *Applied Anatomy and Kinesiology.* Philadelphia: Lea and Febiger, 1937.

Brams, William A. *Managing Your Coronary.* Philadelphia: J. B. Lippincott Company, 1975.

Brodoff, B. N., conf. chm. "Adipose Tissue Metabolism and Obesity Series." *Annals of the New York Academy of Sciences* 131:1–683 (1965).

Brown, Roscoe C., and Gerald S. Kenyon. *Classical Studies on Physical Activity.* Englewood Cliffs, N.J.: Prentice-Hall, 1968.

Brožek, Josef, cons. ed. "Body Composition Series." *Annals of the New York Academy of Sciences* 110:1–124, 425–1018 (1963).

Bruch, Hilde. *The Importance of Overweight.* New York: W. W. Norton & Company, 1957.

Brunner, Daniel, and Ernst Jokl. *Physical Activity and Aging.* Basel: S. Karger, 1970.

Buchwald, Edith. *Physical Rehabilitation for Daily Living.* New York: McGraw-Hill Book Company, 1952.

Cabot, Richard. *Physical Diagnosis.* New York: William Wood and Company, 1927.

Cannon, Walter B. *The Wisdom of the Body.* New York: W. W. Norton & Company, 1963.

————. *Bodily Changes in Pain, Hunger, Fear and Rage.* New York: Harper & Row Torchbooks, 1963.

Chaffee, Ellen E., and Esther M. Greisheimer. *Basic Physiology and Anatomy.* Philadelphia: J. B. Lippincott Company, 1974.

Consolazio, C. Frank. *Physiological Measurements of Metabolic Functions in Man*. New York: McGraw-Hill Book Company, 1963.

Crotty, Bryant J. *Movement Behavior and Motor Learning*. Philadelphia: Lea and Febiger, 1964.

Cureton, Thomas Kirk. *Endurance of Young Men*. Washington, D.C.: Society for Research in Child Development, National Research Council, 1945.

―――. *Physical Fitness Appraisal and Guidance*. St. Louis: The C. V. Mosby Company, 1947.

Curtin, Sharon R. *Nobody Ever Died of Old Age*. Boston: Little, Brown and Company, 1973.

Dawson, Percy M. *The Physiology of Physical Education*. Baltimore: Williams and Wilkins Company, 1935.

Deaver, George G. *Fundamentals of Physical Examination*. Philadelphia: W. B. Saunders Company, 1939.

DeLorme, Thomas L., and Arthur L. Watkins. *Progressive Resistance Exercise*. New York: Appleton-Century-Crofts, 1951.

deRopp, Robert S. *Man Against Aging*. New York: St. Martin's Press, 1960.

deVries, Herbert A. "Measurement and Evaluation of Relaxation." *The Encyclopedia of Sports Medicine*. New York: The Macmillan Company, 1971.

―――. *Vigor Regained*. Englewood Cliffs, N.J.: Prentice-Hall, 1974.

Diserens, Charles M., and Harry Fine. *A Psychology of Music*. Cincinnati, Ohio: College of Music, 1937.

Dobbin, E. Virginia, et al. *The Low Fat, Low Cholesterol Diet*. Garden City, N.Y.: Doubleday & Company, 1951.

English, O. Spurgeon, and Gerald H. J. Pearson. *Common Neuroses of Children and Adults*. New York: W. W. Norton & Company, 1937.

Fleishman, Edwin A. *The Structure and Measurement of Physical Fitness*. Englewood Cliffs, N.J.: Prentice-Hall, 1964.

Forel, August. *Psychotherapy*. New York: Allied Publishing Co., 1927.

Frankel, Lawrence J. "Physical Conditioning Program for Asthmatic Children." *Journal of the American Medical Association* 168:1996–2000 (1958).

———— and Carl J. Roncaglione. "Physical Fitness for the Aging." Paper presented at the Scientific Congress preceding the Olympic Games, München, Germany, 1972.

———— and Ernst Jokl. "Ergometric Fitness Evaluation of 86 Physicians." *American Corrective Therapy Journal* 22:60–67 (1968).

———— and————. Influence of a Sustained Physical Training Regime on Normo and Hypertensive Middle Aged and Old Men. In *Work-Environment-Health: A Collection of Research Reports,* edited by Leo Noro and Thelma Aro 5:24–33. Helsinki: Institute of Occupational Health, 1968.

Glueck, Sheldon, and Eleanor Glueck. *Delinquents in the Making*. New York: Harper & Row, Publishers, 1952.

———— and————. *Physique and Delinquency*. New York: Harper & Row, Publishers, 1956.

Goldthwait, Joel E. *Body Mechanics in Health and Disease*. Philadelphia: J. B. Lippincott Company, 1941.

Halberstam, Michael. *The Pills in Your Life*. New York: Ace Books, 1974.

Harris, Raymond. *The Management of Geriatric Cardiovascular Disease*. Philadelphia: J. B. Lippincott Company, 1970.

230   Hawley, Gertrude. *The Kinesiology of Corrective Exercise*. Philadelphia: Lea and Febiger, 1937.

Health and Fitness in the Modern World. A collection of papers presented at the Institute of Normal Human Anatomy by the Athletic Institute in cooperation with the American College of Sports Medicine. Rome, 1961.

Heckel, Francis. *Cultural Physique*. Paris: Masson et Co., 1913.

Heinz, H. J., Company. *Nutritional Data*. Pittsburgh, Pa.: H. J. Heinz Company, 1956.

Hern, K. M. *Physical Treatment of Injuries of the Brain and Allied Nervous Disorders*. Baltimore: The Williams and Wilkins Company, 1947.

Hettinger, Theodor. *Physiology of Strength*. Springfield, Ill.: Charles C Thomas Publisher, 1961.

Jacobson, Edmund. *Progressive Relaxation*. Chicago: University of Chicago Press, 1974.

Johnson, Warren. *Science and Medicine of Exercise and Sports*. New York: Harper and Brothers, 1960.

Jokl, Ernst. *The Clinical Physiology of Physical Fitness and Rehabilitation*. Springfield, Ill.: Charles C Thomas Publisher, 1971.

———. *Heart and Sport*. Springfield, Ill.: Charles C Thomas Publisher.

———. *Liggaamsoe Feninge-Physical Exercise*. Pretoria, South Africa: J. L. Van Schaik, Ltd.

———. *Medical Sociology and Cultural Anthropology of Sport and Physical Education*. Springfield, Ill.: Charles C Thomas Publisher.

———. *Medicine and Sport*. Lexington, Ky.: University of Kentucky.

———. *Nutrition, Exercise and Body Composition*. Springfield, Ill.: Charles C Thomas Publisher.

———. *Physiology of Exercise*. Springfield, Ill.: Charles C Thomas Publisher, 1971.

————. *Research in Physical Education*. Lexington, Ky.: University of Kentucky.

————. *The Scope of Exercise in Rehabilitation*. Springfield, Ill.: Charles C Thomas Publisher.

————. *What Is Sports Medicine?* Springfield, Ill.: Charles C Thomas Publisher.

———— and P. Jokl. *Exercise and Altitude*. Basel: S. Karger, 1968.

Joslin, Elliott P. *Diabetic Manual*. Philadelphia: Lea and Febiger, 1959.

Jowett, M. A. *The Dialogues of Plato*. National Library Edition. New York: Bigelow, Brown and Company, n.d.

Karvonen, Martti J., et al. *Sports in the Cultural Pattern of the World*. Helsinki: Institute of Occupational Health, 1956.

———— and Alan J. Barry. *Physical Activity and the Heart*. Springfield, Ill.: Charles C Thomas Publisher, 1967.

Klafs, Carl E., and Daniel D. Arnheim. *Modern Principles of Athletic Training*. St. Louis: The C. V. Mosby Company, 1977.

Knudson, K. A., and F. Braae Hansen. *A Text-Book of Gymnastics*. Philadelphia: P. Blakiston's Son & Co., 1937.

Kraus, Hans. *Backache, Stress and Tension*. New York: Simon and Schuster, 1965.

————. *Clinical Treatment of Back and Neck Pain*. New York: McGraw-Hill Book Company, 1970.

————. *Therapeutic Exercises*. Springfield, Ill.: Charles C Thomas Publisher, 1956.

———— and Wilhelm Raab. *Hypokinetic Disease*. Springfield, Ill.: Charles C Thomas Publisher, 1961.

Lamb, Lawrence E. *Your Heart and How to Live with It*. New York: The Viking Press, 1969.

Leaf, Alexander, and John Launois. *Youth in Old Age*. New York: McGraw-Hill Book Company, 1975.

Licht, Sidney. *Therapeutic Exercise*. New Haven, Conn.: Elizabeth Licht, Publisher, 1961.

Lockhart, R. D. *Anatomy of the Human Body*. Philadelphia: J. B. Lippincott Company, 1969.

Lowman, Charles LeRoy, and Carl Haven Young. *Postural Fitness*. Philadelphia: Lea and Febiger, 1963.

McCurdy, A. M. *The Physiology of Exercise*. Philadelphia: Lea and Febiger, 1928.

Mayer, Jean. *Overweight*. Englewood Cliffs, N.J.: Prentice-Hall, 1968.

Menninger, Karl A. *Man Against Himself*. New York: Harcourt, Brace Jovanovich, 1956.

Mensendieck, Bess M. *The Mensendieck System of Functional Exercises*. Portland, Ore.: The Southworth-Antholnsen Press, 1937.

Mercurialis, Hieronymi. Second edition. *De Arte Gymnastica*. Venice. 1573.

Metheny, Eleanor. *Body Dynamics*. New York: McGraw-Hill Book Company, 1952.

Miller, Benjamin F., et al. *Freedom from Heart Attacks*. New York: Simon and Schuster, 1974.

Montagu, Ashley. *Touching*. New York: Columbia University Press, 1971.

Morehouse, Laurence E., and Augustus T. Miller. *Physiology of Exercise*. St. Louis: The C.V. Mosby Company, 1976.

Morrison, Lester. *The Low-Fat Way to Health and Longer Life*. New York: Arco Publishing Co., 1970.

Needles, Robert J. *Your Heart and Common Sense*. New York: Frederick Fell, 1963.

Phelps, Winthrop Morgan. *The Diagnosis and Treatment of Postural Defects*. Springfield, Ill.: Charles C Thomas Publisher, 1932.

Poortmans, J. R. *Biochemistry of Exercise*. Baltimore: University Park Press, 1968.

Prinzmetal, Myron, and William Winter. *Heart Attack: New Hope, New Knowledge, New Life*. New York: Simon and Schuster, 1968.

Raab, Wilhelm. *Prevention of Ischemic Heart Disease*. Springfield, Ill.: Charles C Thomas Publisher, 1966.

Rabinowitz, Dorothy, and Yedida Nielsen. *Home Life*. New York: The Macmillan Company, 1971.

Rasch, Philip J., and Roger K. Burke. *Kinesiology and Applied Anatomy*. Philadelphia: Lea and Febiger, 1974.

Ricci, Benjamin. *Physiological Basis of Human Performance*. Philadelphia: Lea and Febiger, 1969.

Rice, Emmett A. *A Brief History of Physical Education*. New York: The Ronald Press Company, 1958.

Rodahl, Kaare, and Steven Horvath. *Muscle as a Tissue*. New York: McGraw-Hill Book Company, 1962.

————. *Be Fit for Life*. New York: Harper & Row, Publishers, 1966.

Rosenbaum, Francis F., and Elston L. Belknap. *Work and the Heart*. New York: Paul B. Hoeber, 1959.

Rushmer, Robert F. *Cardiovascular Dynamics*. Philadelphia: W. B. Saunders Company, 1976.

Rusk, Howard. *Living with a Disability*. Garden City, N.Y.: The Blakiston Company, 1953.

Schneider, Edward C. *Physiology of Muscular Activity*. Philadelphia: W. B. Saunders Company, 1940.

Selye, Hans. *The Stress of Life*. New York: McGraw-Hill Book Company, 1976.

Sheldon, William H. *Atlas of Men*. New York: Harper & Brothers, 1954.

————. *The Varieties of Delinquent Youth*. New York: Harper & Brothers, 1942.

————. *The Varieties of Human Physique*. New York: Harper & Brothers, 1940.

————. *The Varieties of Temperament*. New York: Harper & Brothers, 1942.

Simon, E., and Ernst Jokl. *International Research in Sport and Physical Education*. Springfield, Ill.: Charles C Thomas Publisher, 1964.

Simonson, Ernst, Conference. *See* Blackburn, Henry.

Smith, Olive F. Guthrie. *Rehabilitation, Re-education and Remedial Exercises*. Baltimore: Williams and Wilkins Company, 1945.

Smout, C.F.V., and R. J. S. McDowall. *Anatomy and Physiology*. Baltimore: Williams & Wilkins Company, 1947.

Spencer, Herbert. *The Principles of Sociology*. Westport: Greenwood Press, 1975.

Stern, Frances. *Applied Dietetics*. Baltimore: Williams and Wilkins Company, 1943.

Strecker, Edward A., and Franklin Ebaugh. *Practical Clinical Psychiatry*. Philadelphia: P. Blakiston's Son and Company, 1931.

Sumption, Dorothy. *Fundamental Danish Gymnastics for Women*. New York: A. S. Barnes and Company, 1932.

Thompson, Clem W. *Manual of Structural Kinesiology*. St. Louis: The C. V. Mosby Company, 1977.

Thulin, J. G.. *Gymnastikatlas*. Stockholm: Svenska Bokforlaget, 1938.

Wells, Harry K., and Ivan P. Pavlov. *Toward a Scientific Psychology and Psychiatry*. New York: International Publishers, 1956.

Westermarck, Edward. *The History of Human Marriage*. New York: The Allerton Book Company, 1922.

Westmann, Stephan K. *Sport, Physical Training and Womanhood*. Baltimore: Williams and Wilkins Company, 1939.

White, Paul Dudley. *My Life and Medicine*. Boston: Gambit, 1971.

Williams, Jesse Feiring. *A Textbook of Anatomy and Physiology*. Philadelphia: W. B. Saunders Company, 1939.

Williams, Marian, and Catherine Worthington. *Therapeutic Exercise for Body Alignment and Function*. Philadelphia: W. B. Saunders Company, 1962.

Index

Abdominal exercises, 28
  in bed, 162, 164, 167–75
  chair, 116–19, 122–28
  combination cardiorespiratory and, 127–28
  double leg circles, 116
  flexed knee sit-up using stall bar, 58
  floor, 56–60, 78–81, 84
  half sit-ups, 59
  rag doll, 117–18
  reverse leg circles, 119
  for sides of waist, 126
  sit-back, 60
  sit-up for the untrained individual, 56
  towel, 167–74
  vigorous, 122–25
Aches and pains, talking about, 212–13
Activity, physical (exercise)
  importance of, 217
  as prescription for good health, 22–23
Aging process, slowing down the, 19
Alley cat routine, 194–95
All fours, exercises on, 78–81
Ankle exercises
  in bed, 163
  chair, 107–9
  flexion and extension, 53, 109
  floor, 52–53
  foot rotations, 52, 107
Arm exercises
  alternate arm extension, 153
  arm circles, 46, 90–91, 101, 154–55
  arm flings, 92, 136–37
  in bed, 153–55, 167–69, 171–74
  chair, 101, 136–37
  floor, 46, 64, 90–92
  towel, 167–69, 171–74
Arthritis, exercises for, 47–51, 102–6, 156–58, 204–5
Åstrand, Per-Olof, 26

Back
  lower, *see* Lower back, exercises for

  upper, exercises for, 64, 78–81
Back arch support, 64
Back problems, 28
Back relaxing exercises, 62–63, 160–61
  dynamic, 120–21
Balance, exercises to improve, 78–81, 84, 188–91, 201–3
Balance beam, 201–3
Bedside gymnastics, 33, 147–81
Bicycling, 127, 164
Blood flow, exercise to stimulate, 144–45
Breathing, 30
Broomstick drills, 71–77, 129–35
  music for, 31
Buttocks, exercise to firm, 82–83

Calf muscles
  exercise for, 144–45
  strengthening, as preparation for walking, 178
Cannon, Walter, 221
Cardiorespiratory exercises, combination abdominal and, 127–28
Carotid pulse, taking, 185
Cat exercise, 78–79
Chair, exercises standing beside, 138–45
Chair exercises, 32, 95–145
Chair straddle, 190–91
Cicero, 214
Coordination, exercise to improve, 201–3
Cross over, 128

Deltoid muscles, exercises for, 44–46, 99–101
Diet, 222–24
Dryden, John, 17

Endurance exercises (interval training), 33, 183–205
  music for, 31
Exercise (physical activity)
  importance of, 217
  as prescription for good health, 22–23

Finger exercises, 200, 204–5
  in bed, 156–57
  chair, 103–6
  finger flexion and extension, 49, 104,
    156
  finger spreading, 50, 105, 157
  finger stretching, 48, 103
  floor, 48–51
  thumb rotations, 51, 106
Fitness, 19–21, 225
Fitness checklist, 27
Fitness programs, as alternatives to
  dependency, 215–6
Flexibility and posture drills for shoulder,
  71–77, 129–35
Flexibility exercises, music for, 31
Floor exercises, 32, 37–93
Floor straddle, 188–89
Foot rotations, 52, 107

Gluteal exercises, 70, 166
Grip exercise, 204–5

Half knee bend, 85
Half sit-ups, 59
Hamstring muscles, exercises for
  in bed, 159
  chair, 115, 138–39
  floor, 38–41, 61, 86–87
Hand exercises, 204–5
  chair, 102, 129–35
  floor, 47, 71–77
  rotations, 47, 102
Head
  raising, 149
  turning, 150
Head back and forward, 42, 97
Head turned to look over shoulder, 43, 98
Heart rate, 184–87
  immediate, 186
  resting, 186
  suggestions for taking, 185
  target, 186–87
Hemorrhoidal conditions, exercise for, 70
Hip exercises
  in bed, 164, 165, 175
  chair, 140
  floor, 65–67, 93
Hip raising, 175
Hip rotations, 93
Hippocrates, 22

Hook lying, 209–10
Hyperextension exercise, 68–69

Inactivity, 217
Interval training exercises for endurance,
  33, 183–205
  music for, 31

Knee bend
  half, 85
  partial, 142
Knee flexion, extension, and scale, 80–81
Knee to chest, 62, 63, 84, 143, 160, 161
Kraus, Hans, 34
Kreitler, Hans, 217
Kreitler, S., 217

Laughter, 221
Leg circles
  double, 116
  reverse, 119
Leg lunging, 82–83
Leg raising, 65, 159
  from side-lying position, 165
Leg swinging
  forward and backward, 140
  side, 141
Low back pain, 28
Lower back, exercises for
  in bed, 160–61, 175
  chair, 117–18
  floor, 38–41, 62–63, 68–69, 78–81,
    84, 86–87
Lying-down position (recumbent position),
  29

Mayer, Jean, 222
Medical examination, 26, 27
Medicine ball, 208
Mental processes, activity and, 217
Mental stimulation, 19–20, 214
Montagu, Ashley, 219
Music, 221
  background, 25, 31, 194, 197

Neck exercises
  in bed, 149–50
  chair, 97–98
  ear toward shoulder, 43, 98
  floor, 42–43
  head back and forward, 42, 97

head turned to look over shoulder, 43, 98
Nutrition, 222

Obesity, 223

Pains, talking about, 213–14
Physician, examination by, 26, 27, 183
Plato, 221
Posture and flexibility drills for shoulder,
   71–77, 129–35
Pulse, *see* Heart rate

Quadriceps exercises, 113–14, 170

Radial pulse, taking, 185
Rag doll, 86–87, 117–18
Range of motion exercises, music for, 31
Rectal sphincter, exercises to improve
   circulation in, 70, 166
Recumbent position, 29
Relaxation exercises, 207–10
   music for, 31
Rocking chair, 219–20
Rodahl, Kaare, 26
Rope skipping, 196–97

Scale (position), 80–81
Schopenhauer, Arthur, 212
Scissors kick, 66, 128
Self-image, 217
Self-respect, 212
Serenity, technique for, 209–10
Shock, Nathan, 18
Shoulder, posture and flexibility drills for,
   71–77, 129–35
Shoulder exercises
   alternate arm extension, 154
   arm circles, 46, 90–91, 101, 154–55
   arm flings, 92, 136
   in bed, 151–55, 171–73
   chair, 99–101, 136
   floor, 44–46, 90–92
   shoulder rotations, 45, 100, 152
   shoulder shrugs, 44, 99, 151

towel, 171–73
Side bends, 88–89
Side-lying exercises, 65–67
Side stretch, 67
Sit-back, 60
Sitting position, 29
Sit-ups
   half, 59
   for the untrained individual, 56
   using stall bar, flexed knee, 58
Smiling, 221
Spine, exercises for upper, 42–43, 68–69,
   78–81, 97–99, 149–50
Standing exercises, 82–93
   music for, 31
Step bench exercise, 192–93
Straddle exercises, 188–91
   chair, 190–91
   floor, 188–89
Stretching exercises, 38–41
   alternate stretching, 38–39
   legs together, 41
   reaching through center, 40

Tension, exercises to release, 207–10
Thigh muscles, exercises for
   in bed, 165, 170
   chair, 110–14, 142
   floor, 54–55, 65–67, 82–83, 85
   towel, 170
Thigh muscles, strengthening, as
   preparation for walking, 176–78
Thumb rotations, 51, 106, 158
Towel exercises, 167–74

Waist muscles, side-of-, exercises for,
   65–67, 88–89, 165
   abdominal, 126
Walking, 179–81, 218
   preparation for, 176–78
Weight control, 223–24
Wrist exercises, 47, 102

Youthfulness, 214